DATE DUE			

John D. Young
and the
Colorado Gold Rush

The Lakeside Classics

JOHN D. YOUNG
AND THE
COLORADO GOLD RUSH

EDITED BY

DWIGHT L. SMITH

The Lakeside Press

R. R. DONNELLEY & SONS COMPANY

CHICAGO

Christmas, 1969

PUBLISHERS' PREFACE

THE lure of gold played a significant role in opening the West to settlement as well as providing a financial base for America's growth during the 19th century. It is only natural that this intriguing metal which has excited man since antiquity would also inspire numerous stories about the search for gold.

The Lakeside Classics has published narratives on the California Gold Rush of '49 and, recently, Jeremiah Lynch's story about the Klondike district of the Yukon near the close of the 19th century.

This year we trace the journey of John D. Young and his party from Chicago to the gold fields of Colorado in 1860. This book represents a departure from most of those in our series. In most instances we have used out-of-print books as source materials. However, our narrative this year is from an unpublished journal which is in the collection of The Newberry Library in Chicago.

The Newberry Library was endowed by Walter Loomis Newberry and has been a rich repository of the humanities since its founding in 1887. Scholars from all over the world come to Chicago to carry out research in the humanities from the priceless collections of this renowned library.

We are also indebted to Colton Storm of Sedona, Arizona, one of our Consulting Editors, who suggested this unpublished journal. The task of seeking suitable first-person narratives relating to American history is a challenging one. We appreciate the research and assistance of our Consulting Editors, and we always welcome suggestions of possible manuscripts from our readers.

A short time after John D. Young's manuscript was presented to The Newberry Library, Dwight L. Smith, Research Professor of History at Miami University in Oxford, Ohio, examined it and expressed a strong desire to study the text. Fortunately, we were able to engage Dr. Smith, a specialist in frontier American and Canadian history, to edit this first edition and provide the Historical Introduction and footnotes that will enable the reader to fully appreciate the author's account.

Our author, John D. Young, maintained his good spirits throughout his narrative even while describing the deprivation and disappointment his party faced. It is the story of a loser who waited two years after the first announcement of gold in Colorado to begin his quest. His best day in the gold fields yielded less than his daily expenses and most surely hastened his return to Chicago.

His party departed Chicago just a month before Lincoln's nomination as the Republican candidate at the Wigwam in Chicago in May 1860. His return in September found the United States moving inexorably closer to the events that culminated in the Civil War. It is perhaps not surprising that he did not chronicle these events, since his account is confined to a description of his journey over the five-month period.

We are experiencing a strong demand for many of our services, including catalogs and other gravure printing, telephone directories, and certain categories of magazines. At the time this is written, it is impossible to forecast accurately the sales and profits for our Company this year, due in part to anticipated costs of the surtax and start-up expenses of new operations, as well as to unexpected casualty losses and lost production suffered in the September explosion and fire in our Chicago gravure pressroom.

This was a trying period—not only to the families of those of our employees who lost their lives and to those who were injured—but to the hundreds of our employees who worked long hours for many weeks to get the damaged facilities back into production to serve our customers' needs.

We are proud of our people's response to this tragedy—of the selfless acts of heroism in rescuing fellow workers and fighting the fire and of the hundreds of people who have pulled together to re-open the plant or worked long hours to produce customer work in other locations. We were supported greatly by the prompt response and fine work of Chicago's fire and police units and hospitals in the area. Chicago fire officials paid tribute to the training and experience of our employees and the construction of the plant as contributing factors in reducing the number of injuries.

We are grateful also for the support and patience of our customers and suppliers who helped us in adjusting schedules and expediting construction and repair efforts.

We are planning for continued growth and the technological challenges of the future. This requires the recruitment and development of people to fulfill a wide range of craft, staff, and managerial responsibilities. Training programs take on an increasing significance in the development of skills which will enable us to adapt to the ever-changing demands of technology and organization. These programs make it possible, for the most part, to maintain our long-standing practice of promotion from within.

We have made organizational changes to meet our growth requirements and enable us to better serve our customers. Until recently, our manufacturing was divided into a number of separate divisions with some individual staff services, but sales and other staff services were retained at the corporate level. Recently two groups have been formed—one for books, another for magazines. Each group is headed by a senior vice president and consists of several manufacturing divisions and a sales organization. They rely on the corporate office for many staff services.

Our Research and Development program, the largest in our industry, strives to keep us in the forefront in the development and use of more sophisticated methods, processes and tools.

In looking to the future we anticipate the need for new manufacturing divisions in various parts of the country. We are preparing for this by searching out sites and, in some cases, obtaining options for or buying land with no specific plans for its use. This land inventory shortens considerably the necessarily long period required for customer contract negotiation, building and equipping a plant, recruiting and training a work force, and actual start-up of operations. A good example of this is our new division in Glasgow, Kentucky, which will commence producing special interest magazines by the middle of 1970.

We sincerely hope our many friends share our confidence about our future. It is you—our customers, suppliers, employees and friends—whose past confidence and cooperation have provided the base for our past success, and for our future plans.

May we wish all of you a bright future, a Merry Christmas, and a Happy New Year.

THE PUBLISHERS

Christmas, 1969

CONTENTS

ILLUSTRATIONS

HISTORICAL INTRODUCTION

FIRED up by the exhilarating experience of the 1849 gold rush to California and conditioned by the economic distress in the wake of the panic of 1857, it is not surprising that the exciting news out of the South Platte River country of western Kansas Territory electrified the American people in 1858. The victims of the virus would be numbered in the scores of thousands.

The presence of gold had long been imagined or known of in the Rocky Mountain country. Its incidence and availability had been the subject matter of rumors, exaggerations, factual accounts, and the wishful thinking of the Indians, Mexicans, and Spanish for centuries. This had motivated prodding and searching and intrigue of all kinds. But the geography was confusing and the stuff was elusive.

While miners are like fishermen who are most reluctant to reveal their favorite fishing holes, they are also like little boys who can hardly wait to share their secrets with others. Discoveries were made, the secret was out, and the news spread miraculously, even in the absence of modern means of communication. Remember, the Pony Express was not instituted until 1860 and the electric telegraph did not span the continent until the next year.

In the summer of 1858 rumors traveled eastward that substantial strikes were being made in the Pike's

Peak area.[1] Convinced that it was merely a matter of time before the precious stuff would be uncovered in profitable quantities, a real estate spree resulted in the establishment of what was to become Denver to handle the anticipated influx of business and settlers.

On August 26, 1858, the Kansas City *Journal of Commerce* proclaimed "The New Eldorado!!! Gold in Kansas Territory!!" The story, appearing within a few days in newspapers all the way to the east coast, was that nine mountaineers "just in" "this morning" from Pike's Peak had brought the evidence with them, the fineness of which "equals the choicest of California specimens." One man reported he had dug his pay dirt with an ax and then had washed it out with a frying pan. Kansas City, it was asserted, "is alive with excitement, and parties are already preparing for the diggings." Helpfully, the area was located and the readers were informed that game, timber, water, and grass were plentiful. Other travelers and news soon began to come into the Missouri settlements with newspapers giving exciting coverage.[2]

[1] Although there is still considerable room for research on the history of the Colorado gold rush, solid beginnings have been made. This brief sketch has been obtained, principally, from LeRoy R. Hafen, ed., *Colorado Gold Rush: Contemporary Letters and Reports, 1858–1859* (Glendale, California, 1941); Charles W. Henderson, *Mining in Colorado: A History of Discovery, Development and Production* (U. S. Geological Survey, *Professional Paper 138*, Washington, 1926). References to other materials are made in subsequent footnotes.

Previous accounts had been ill-founded and exaggerated and generally were given scant attention. The late August newspaper notice from Kansas City was different. It was confirmed by the pouches of the yellow dust which the men had brought back with them. Within a few weeks gold seekers were heading westward from Missouri. Some, of course, returned discouraged, denouncing the whole business as a promotional scheme of real estate speculators. A substantial enough number wintered at the base of the mountains and sent back sufficiently encouraging letters to confirm the tantalizing authenticity of a New Eldorado in the minds of thousands back in the States.

That the gold was there was a well established fact. But it had only been found in stream sand and gravel in insufficient quantities to make it worthwhile. When John H. Gregory, "the Sutter of the Rocky Mountains," uncovered a quartz vein, an outcrop of a gold lode, on May 6, 1859, it was a new story.

The Gregory diggings, near present Central City, was followed by the discovery of other rich placer deposits and lodes. For the rest of the year and through the next, most of the central Rockies area was searched. There was a steady stream of "fifty-

---

[2]Although disputed by some, this newspaper article is generally credited as the first consequential account of the Colorado gold discovery to the outside world. It, and other relevant documents are reprinted in Hafen, *Colorado Gold Rush*, 19–21, 30–32, *et passim.*

niners" hurrying westward to the Pike's Peak country, and, inevitably, hundreds of discouraged and unsuccessful ones returning homeward in the other direction.

Among the numerous reports and accounts that helped to authenticate the idea that there was indeed a pot of gold at the end of the rainbow were the efforts of three journalists. In the summer of 1859, Cincinnati, Boston, and New York newspapers dispatched their ablest to visit the Gregory diggings while their readers breathlessly awaited firsthand accounts. No less a person than Horace Greeley, renowned editor of the New York *Tribune*, represented his paper. Their dispatches, appearing also in book form, rang with authority, and must be credited with a sizable share of the excitement and motivation involved in the Pike's Peak gold rush.[3]

Production figures are hard to come by for these early years, and, at best, are estimates. The value of the bullion, chiefly gold, from Colorado mines, that was deposited in the Philadelphia mint and the government assay office in New York City was:

[3] Horace Greeley, *An Overland Journey, from New York to San Francisco, in the Summer of 1859* (New York, 1860), 115–127, 139–148; Albert D. Richardson, *Beyond the Mississippi . . . 1857–1867* (Hartford, 1867), 179–203; and Henry Villard, *The Past and Present of the Pike's Peak Gold Regions* (St. Louis, 1860. Reprinted by LeRoy Hafen, ed., Princeton, 1932). A useful bibliography in this connection is Henry R. Wagner, *The Plains and the Rockies: A Bibliography of Original Narratives of Travel and Adventure, 1800–1865* (Revised and extended by Charles L. Camp, San Francisco, 1937).

$4,172.00 for the year beginning June 30, 1859; and $599,846.00 for the following year. If, as a rule of thumb for the first decade of Colorado production, the amount of these deposits " 'embraces only one-third of the total product of the mines,' " then an estimated 1.8 million dollars worth of the yellow metal was extracted or panned in these two first years. Eventually Colorado would yield well over a billion dollars[3] worth of gold and silver! Although production peaked in later years, further detailed statistical data is not here pertinent.[4]

Among the thousands who were trekking it westward to the gold fields in the summer of 1860 was a youthful Chicagoan by the name of John D. Young. Although he did not find the pot of gold at the end of the rainbow, his account of the adventure enriches the literature of that momentous page of western history.

Only the sketchiest of biographical data is available on Young. It is known that he was born in Canada on May 1, 1839, of Irish parents who settled in Chicago in 1843. The precise identity of "the graded schools and State University" in which he was educated remains evasive.

Young moved to Ottawa, Illinois, in 1863 and secured employment as a clerk. Four years later, he

[4]Henderson, *Mining in Colorado*, 69, 71, 249. Colorado gold output alone, through 1965, was about 40,776,000 ounces. At $35.00 an ounce this amounts to some 1.4 billion dollars. News Release, Geological Survey, Department of Interior, Washington, December 13, 1968, page 3.

and another man were able to buy out the proprietors and to establish a partnership for themselves.
Lumber merchant Young was actively interested in
civic affairs. In 1881 he was elected to serve a one-
year term as mayor of his city. At his death on
February 21, 1898, he was survived by his widow
and seven children who moved to Chicago shortly
after that.[5]

Young was one of a party of seven, including one
of his brothers and his father, that left Chicago in
mid-April 1860 on the Chicago, Burlington, and
Quincy Railroad, for an overnight ride to the Mississippi River town of Quincy.[6] By river steamer the
group went downstream to Hannibal, Missouri, and
from thence on the Hannibal and St. Joseph Railroad across Missouri. Reflecting on the river-valley-
confined settlements of that state Young conjectured that its growth and prosperity would come in
a post-slavery era. St. Joseph, Missouri, was a sur-

[5] U. J. Hoffman, *History of LaSalle County, Illinois* (Chicago, 1906), 566–567, 1102; Ottawa, Illinois, City Council
Record Book #2, page 5; obituary, Ottawa *Republican-Times,*
February 24, 1898; undated [1918] obituary of Mrs. Young
from Ottawa newspaper.

[6] The names of the members of the party are given in the
Denver *Rocky Mountain Herald*, May 26, 1860, as: John
Young, J. D. Young, James Young, J. M. Mullen, M. Kerwin,
T. Conners, and J. Hennessy.

J[ohn] D. Young's younger brother was James Young and
his father was John Young. These identities are determined
from the federal census records of 1850, Inhabitants in Chicago 4th Ward, County of Cook, State of Illinois, Vol. 4,
p. 523.

prisingly sophisticated city to be located so far out on the western frontier. And the departure and arrival of the Pony Express furnished fascination and excitement.

Since the real purpose of the venture was into the golden West, Young and his fellow travelers crossed the wide Missouri River by ferry to the Kansas Territory town of Bellemont and headed into the Great Plains. Across the northeast corner of Kansas and into southeastern Nebraska they came to the Platte River at Grand Island. Their route from St. Joseph westward, proclaimed by one guide book as "the nearest, cheapest, and most expeditious" one to the Pike's Peak country, was called "the Great Platte Valley Route."[7]

Although the great outdoors whetted their appetites, and a singing contest with Kansas girls was great fun, the rough going in the bluff country of the Missouri River valley dampened their spirits. The flora and the fauna and the absence of these things gave them variety and concern. The city boys were taken to the tune of seven pieces of silver to view a withered one-hundred-and-twenty-year-old Indian who had once been a powerful chief and a great warrior. Some of their evenings around the campfire were livened by story telling and flute accompanied singing.

[7] *1859. 1859. Traveler's Guide to the New Gold Mines in Kansas and Nebraska, with a Description of the Shortest and Most Direct Route from Chicago to Pike's Peak & Cherry Creek Gold Mines* (Polhemus & de Vries, New York, 1859),7.

From Grand Island along the Platte, monotony was interspersed with adventure. An abundance of game, water, and wood alternated with a serious lack thereof. Young assessed Fort Kearney's location as strategically unfortunate; and its troops were superbly trained but shabbily clothed. Starving Indians hounded the party; they were so desperately hungry that they ravenously ate horses that dropped dead along the road.

After the forks of the Platte, the route followed the south branch of the river on to Denver and the mining country. Recently explored and opened, however, was a cutoff road that left the South Platte near present Brush in northeastern Colorado, and followed in a more direct way to Denver than by the river. It was proclaimed as safe and bountiful in supplies as well as offering a substantial saving in miles.

Although Young was skeptical of the accounts of abundance of sustaining water, fuel, and grass along the cutoff, although he was fearful of the probability of hostile Indians, and although his party had repeatedly decided to stay on the Platte road, when they reached the cutoff Young alone opposed taking it. It was nearly a fatal decision even though over forty other emigrants banded together with them for this final leg of the journey into Denver. They were threatened by "more than a thousand . . . wild devils." Fortunately the strategy of the travelers, the cowardice of the warriors, or something else kept the savages from attacking.

By contrast, their next encounter with the Indians was with a friendly group with whom they traded goods and indulged in athletic prowess and contests. This, a prairie dog city, and the majestic Rocky Mountains on the horizon changed their mood as they approached a phenomenal and exciting new experience, the urban frontier of Denver.

Not yet two years old, Denver was destined to be more than just a mere flash in the pan, the fate of so many other mining camps. It was already well on the way to sophistication and maturity beyond its tender years. The prairie-worn travelers marveled at its wonders and exciting atmosphere. A businessman friend gave them an intimate tour. By chance a saloon-brawl murder occurred within hearing distance and they attended the lynch-law trial and execution of the culprit.

Real adventure and danger were still ahead of them as they left the town for the gold fields of the Continental Divide country to the south and the west. Traveling was extremely difficult and trying. Getting lost in the wilderness was fearsome. Exhaustion from near starvation, an encampment of hostile Indians, a forest fire, and a near catastrophic encounter with mountain wolves were among the dangers that nearly doomed them. Nor was humor lacking, as when his goggle-eyed mule awakened and startled Young by breathing on his face in the middle of a cold night in the mountain wilds. The poor critter was lonely!

With all of this and more, they did reach the gold fields at Tarryall. Leaving one member of their group to mind camp, horses, provisions, and some equipment, the others fanned out in pairs to mining districts to prospect their potential. Young and his companion went across the Divide to the Blue River diggings, and along California Gulch of the upper Arkansas River country. His description of the various mining techniques, of mining frontier law and justice and defense, of claims and salting, of mining camps, and of water supply problems are intimate and graphic.

He witnessed a conference between the Indians and the miners in which the former pleaded for recognition of their rights and property. The Indians spoke so eloquently and convincingly that he was ready to champion their rights. Though he spoke of "greeny" with understanding, he was gullible enough to participate in a hoax rush that roused him from bed in the middle of the night and took him over a dangerous mountain pass to a fruitless strike.

By the time all the party returned to Tarryall they had concluded that "the whole thing was a humbug and that we had better get out of the place as soon as possible." The fever had infected them more than they were willing to admit, however. On the morning of their expected departure it was reported that gold was discovered on the very gulch in which they were camping. So they joined the excitement, staked out claims, and went to work.

It took three days to make a tailing ditch and to divert the stream bed and three more days to reach pay dirt eleven feet below. The first day's work of washing pay dirt netted them the magnificent sum of three dollars, about forty-three cents apiece. Over two weeks the amount varied to as high as seventy cents a day per man. With their expenses of about a dollar a day, they at last concluded to call it quits. Young considered himself fortunate to find a buyer for his claim for five dollars.

After selling their mining tools and excess provisions and other supplies, four of the group changed their minds and decided to stay awhile longer to give it "one more trial." The remaining three were joined by three more friends for the return trip, one of whom apparently went no further with them than Denver.

Things were exciting and tense when Young's group finally got back to town. The Ute and the Sioux had battled it out a few days before and thousands of Sioux had come to Denver. Although the town fathers agreed to militia assistance if the Sioux were attacked, in return for an agreement to camp a few miles down the river, their proximity was cause for apprehension. The all-night scalp dance and the burning at the stake of one of their prisoners did not allay the fears of the local populace. A delegation of citizens persuaded the Indians to surrender the other prisoner, a young squaw who most certainly would have been subjected to the same fate. The town breathed much easier when the Sioux moved on.

Denver in the summer of 1860 was vibrant. Two principal developments contributed to this tremendous outpouring of energy and activity. The first consisted of the still fantastic immigration whose temporary goal was Denver as the unofficial headquarters of the Pike's Peak gold rush ("Pike's Peak" should be translated as "Colorado") and the increasing exodus of the discouraged and disillusioned who concluded that the pot of gold at the end of the rainbow was all humbug. Not very many of those returning to the States were willing to look at it philosophically, writing it off as an exciting experience. Although discouraged, Young tended to belong to that few. Transient crowds restlessly milled about in the streets waiting impatiently to move on to the gold fields or to get back East. The two-way movement became even more evident out on the trail on the way back home.

The second development that explains the energized and supercharged atmosphere of 1860 Denver, closely related to the first, was the growing pains of urbanization. The efforts to control the mining frontier and to accommodate the growing number of transients, as well as the need to provide for the concomitant increase in population, made for flux and ferment. Young sensed the drama of which he was a part and makes some interesting observations, especially on the social and legal aspects and the changing nature of mining itself as mechanization became a necessity.

Young and his four companions hit the influx-exodus trail in early July. Instead of using the Beaver Creek cutoff from Denver they left town along the older Platte River trail. Except for this variation, the return to Chicago was over much the same route as the one they had come out on. Even though water-less, wood-less, and grass-less days on end were nearly disastrously monotonous, the wearisome sameness of the journey was punctuated with occasional excitement and danger.

Although they knew better, they offered whisky to an Indian who replenished their meat supply. His fellow tribesmen became quite unfriendly when they were refused a drink so that they too could become drunkenly sick. The hungry travelers welcomed the chance to kill a buffalo but were nearly literally overwhelmed by the endless sea of the critters as the herd was thundering across their path in its seasonal migration. The thousands of mounds marking the last resting places of gold rushers who never completed their journeys were unpleasant reminders of the hazards of such a trip. Mosquitoes were an unwelcome embellishment as the party plodded eastward across the plains. One of their horses gave out and had to be abandoned. And the day after they passed through Marysville, Kansas, a prairie twister blew it off the map.

On the way westward Young had talked about flute playing and singing, storytelling, and athletic contests with friendly Indians, as diversions. The mood of the homeward journey did not encourage such lightheartedness. Young does mention a tried and true antidote to the prevailing melancholy. To conserve the waning strength of horses and humans during the heat of the prairie day they sought shady places to rest. In these hours, he read pamphlet copies of the works of Sir Walter Scott which he had with him. "I believe I should have died of the blues but for them."

Eventually they reached "the borders of civilization." Sunburned, ragged clothes, virtually barefoot, with five months' hair and beards, they plunged into the comparative luxuries and amenities of things nearly forgotten. Even knives and forks now seemed strange. After four days in St. Joseph, they entrained for Chicago thus ending their adventure of five months and two days.

John D. Young kept a vivid record of his adventures of the summer of 1860. It is a detailed narrative portraying the excitement of a young man out to strike it rich in the gold fields of the West. It is a first-hand account of his experiences of overland travel, a portrayal of young Denver, life in the precarious gold camps of Colorado, and the return home.

With no explanation from Young, the circumstances of its composition and writing can only be guessed. Since the manuscript journal is not in the form of daily diary entries but rather cast as a continuous narrative, it is unlikely that he composed it while on the journey. He may have written chunks of it at various times during his travels and experiences, and re-copied them after he returned home. Either this or complete composition, perhaps from

notes after he was back in Chicago, seem likely con-
jectures. The details and the immediacy of his writing are such that it is almost certain he at least kept
notes and perhaps a rough draft while he was under-
going the experiences.

Although Young is given to romanticizing and at
times to slight exaggeration these things do not
spoil or discredit his story. Considering the heavy in-
dulgence of distortion and propaganda that charac-
terized many guide books and newspaper accounts,
it is a wonder that there is not considerably more of
this in what Young writes. Allowance must be made
for some error that creeps in, but with the tremendous amount of misinformation that had currency,
his errors are largely inadvertent rather than deliber-
ate distortion. These things do not detract from
Young's telling of his adventures with all the youthful impressions and exuberance that he includes.

The Young manuscript is written in pencil and
ink on 120 pages of legal-size paper, some lined and
some unlined. The script is generally very readable,
but some pages are exceedingly dim, nearly defying
transcription. Identification of its author is made on
the bottom of page 37 where he wrote his name. On
the top of the first page is the heading: "A trip to
the gold regions of the Rocky Mountains in the summer of 1860."

As Young produced it one sentence follows
another frequently without capitalization of the first
word or terminal punctuation the sentences roll
along page after page without any interruption in

one one hundred and twenty page paragraph that leaves the reader breathless and exhausted.

For the sake of readability but without violation of his composition, reproduction of his text is faithful with the following editorial modifications: The text lends itself to six logical subdivisions; chapter titles are provided for these. Paragraphing is introduced. Inconsistent capitalization is corrected especially as it applies to the first word of a sentence. Young is sparing and erratic with his punctuation. In instances where the manuscript is not clear, transcription is made into the appropriate marks; but, except for terminal punctuation, none is introduced. Young's disturbing omission of terminal punctuation is corrected with the use of the editorial virgule or slanting line/ The frequent necessity for use of this device makes it commonplace enough to be acceptable rather than serving as an obstacle to readability. Apostrophes for possessives and periods for abbreviations are introduced silently. Pikes Peak is spelled with an apostrophe by Young and in numerous publications of the period. Largely because of Young's penchant for phonetic spelling, his numerous errors are corrected to obviate the employment of [*sic*] with annoying frequency.

Only occasional editorial explanation or identification is supplied in notes because the narrative is generally self explanatory. To do otherwise would detract from the story as Young so aptly and interestingly tells it.

Preparing the Young manuscript for publication

has involved the combined and cooperative efforts of several persons. First is the late Mrs. Blanche Young Warren, Young's last surviving child. Her father's journal was being used in the classroom by her niece, a California school teacher. Mrs. Warren obtained a photostatic copy of the journal which she offered to Colton Storm, then Head of the Department of Special Collections at The Newberry Library. Storm expressed enthusiastic interest in the journal and stated his conviction that the original should be in the Library archives and the sturdier photostatic copy used for classroom purposes. One tornadic Chicago day after this discussion, octogenarian Mrs. Young walked into the Library and presented the original manuscript and literary rights to it as a gift.

I am everlastingly grateful to Colton Storm for encouraging me to confirm his high praise and enthusiasm for Young's account. Newberry's Lawrence W. Towner, Director, granted me permission to prepare it for publication. James M. Wells, Associate Director, and Matt P. Lowman II, Head, Department of Special Collections at Newberry, have aided me in many ways including the use of the considerable research materials of the Library.

Mrs. Enid T. Thompson, Librarian, and Mrs. Kathleen Pierson, and Don L. Davidson, Division of Photographs, State Historical Society of Colorado; Mrs. Irene R. Reinka, Head, Reference Department, Reddick's Library, Ottawa, Illinois; and Miss Janet Fairbanks, Office of the Mayor, Ottawa,

Illinois, have done special chores for me. I am indebted to Miami University, Oxford, Ohio, for released time for the project, and to its Library for use of collateral reference materials. Charles C. Kerwin and Edward M. Kerwin of Chicago, and Thomas J. Kerwin of Denver, son, son, and grandson, respectively, of Michael W. Kerwin who was a member of Young's party in 1860, gave helpful counsel and advice and furnished vital information.

Special credit is due to Rodney Chirpe, of Chicago, the creative cartographer who produced the maps and, from a publication of the period, the frontispiece for this volume. The other illustrations are used with the permission and the courtesy of the State Historical Society of Colorado.

Two others who helped ease the burden of the back-breaking drudgery must be singled out. My wife, Jane D. Smith, spent countless hours collating and reading proof through the various stages of the project. Mrs. Patricia J. McGuire patiently typed and typed and typed, a chore that tends to dull the excitement and interest of any publication venture.

Finally, much credit is due the members of the R. R. Donnelley & Sons Company staff who have crafted my efforts into one of *The Lakeside Classics*.

DWIGHT L. SMITH

Oxford, Ohio, 1969

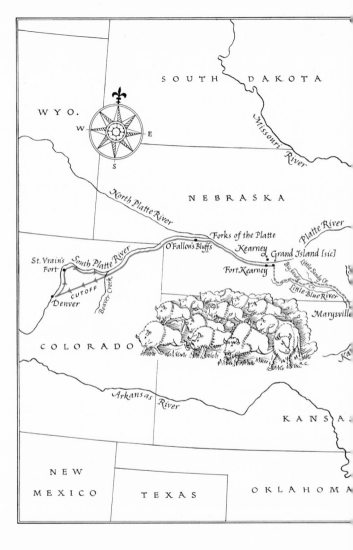

CODE

+++++ RAILROADS
~~~~~ ROUTE
- - - PROBABLE ROUTE

JOHN D. YOUNG'S

ROUTE

John D. Young
and the
Colorado Gold Rush

Chapter I

Westward to Eldorado:
Chicago to Denver

EXCITEMENT was running very high in the summer of 1860 in respect to the gold regions of Kansas and Nebraska. Almost every man who could raise the means gave up his business and prospects in the states and started for the land of gold expecting to realize a fortune in one short summer. Having perhaps the same foolish views of the rest of the young men of our place, I determined to make one of the crowd bound for the new Eldorado of the West. Accordingly we raised a party consisting of seven persons, bought arms and equipments, and embarked on our long and tedious journey.[1] We started on the [Chicago,] Burlington and Quincy Railroad running through the center of the state the most fertile and best settled part, and let me here remark that on this land is by far the best land in the West/* At the time I traveled through there they had a most splendid harvest. The grain was full and yellow and

*This virgule or slanting line is an editorial device to correct Young's frequent omission of terminal punctuation.

[1]Lacking dated and precise daily entries, it is necessary to use internal evidence to establish the time of the expedition. Two firm dates are mentioned by Young. He departed from Denver on the return trip on Friday, July 1. This date cannot

3

as I afterwards was informed so vast was the crop
that they could not ship it and were compelled to
make fuel of it.

On the following morning we arrived at Quincy
on the Mississippi River one of the most ancient
towns in Illinois. It is a town of considerable importance having beautiful facilities for trading on the
upper and lower Mississippi and with the interior
of Illinois and Missouri. The streets here are very
irregular there being no attempt towards a uniformity
of grade/ The door sill of one house sometimes is on
a level with the roof of a neighboring house some
three or [four?] stories in height/ It is very unpleasant and dreadfully tiresome. The Mississippi at

be used because of vague references to time before and afterwards.

The other date is May 5 when the party passed through
Fort Kearney on the outward journey. If his days before this
are all accounted for, as they seem to be, on or about April 17
was the date of departure from Chicago. Using this and assuming that his closing remark that the entire venture took
five months and two days is accurate, the party apparently
arrived back in Chicago on or about September 18.

The manuscript overland diary of Michael William Kerwin
who went to the Pike's Peak gold country in 1860 is in The
Newberry Library. That he was a member of Young's party
(see Introduction) is confirmed by the roster notice of the
arrival of the group in a Denver newspaper. Although Kerwin and J. M. Mullen (Joseph McMullen in Kerwin's diary)
and two others did not return to the East with Young,
Kerwin's diary does furnish some basis for checking and con-
firming Young's narrative. According to Kerwin, the group
left Chicago on April 16. With uncertainty in some of Kerwin's later dates in the diary, this one may or may not be
accurate.

this point is a magnificent looking sight, It is about a mile wide the water of a sky blue color and remarkably clear, The beautiful islands [are] dotting its surface for miles above and below its green shores rising into bold rocky bluffs many hundred feet in height and covered with the bright green color of spring. It was indeed a beautiful scene and one that I shall never forget, The great father of water was clothed in all its splendor and grandeur.

On the following morning we embarked on its broad bosom on board the steamer Pike, a splendid specimen of a Mississippi River boat large as the huge leviathans that plow furrows in the broad Atlantic, Her cabins [are] a magnificent palace, Altogether one of those boats can compare favorably with the floating craft of any country. And now all being ready we steamed up the noble river passing by fairy looking islands that it would not take a great stretch of the imagination to suppose they were inhabited by the spirits of the red men who lived for ages on its shores. Passing by rapidly all these scenes the steamer suddenly rounded to come up to the levee and we were at the landing of the city of Hannibal, Missouri.

We disembarked and proceeded to view the town, We found it to be a nicely situated town containing about four thousand inhabitants. It is situated on the river bottoms parallel with the river and between its banks and the bluffs which are here many hundred feet in height. The city has an appearance of business, There are a number of quite respectable looking stores which seem to be doing quite a thriving business. Here I first seen slavery/ There are a few Negroes in the city/ Its proximity to the Illinois shore prevents the holding of slaves to any great extent. We stopped in this town only a very short time and once more started on the iron horse bound for the far off shores of the Missouri.

I must here make some remarks about the interior of Missouri/ It is a splendid looking farming country, nice rolling land fine streams of pure clear water, and a small quantity of timber/ Altogether a most splendid farming country yet between Hannibal and St. Joe about two hundred and fifty miles there is scarcely the sign of a well cultivated farm/ You will think this very strange that people should pass such fine land so near a market, and go and locate in such out of the way places, as Kansas and Nebraska, but the reason is simple/ It is because it is a slave state. A northern man cannot go there and take a farm because they are averse to holding slaves and if he works his farm himself he is looked upon with scorn by his neighbor who works his farm by slaves/ He is constantly taunted with being poor white trash and it annoys him so that he leaves in disgust and moves to some country where honest labor is not looked upon as a disgrace by the nabobs of the South. This is the only reason why this beautiful and fertile state is only settled along the river shores/ Slavery is not a paying institution there consequently there is no danger of its spreading north as many of our northern people are afraid of. Nature has erected barriers against slavery more potent than any that could be enacted by Congress. As soon as slavery is abolished in Missouri then will she take her stand along with her sister states the richest and proudest of all.

One day's ride on the railroad brought us clear across the state of Missouri into the city of St. Joe,[2] the furthest north western city of the United States. It is situated on the banks of the river partly on the bottoms and partly on the bluffs. One would be surprised at finding such a large fine looking city away so far from civilization, It has a compact well built and substantial appearence, Many of its buildings would compare favorably with the finest of our own great city, The Patee House is as large as the Tremont House,[3] It is situated on the outskirts of the city on slightly elevated ground commanding a beautiful view of the Missouri River. From this house the Pony Express starts for California,

[2]The Hannibal and St. Joseph R.R. made the trip across Missouri in twelve hours. *1859. 1859. Traveler's Guide to the New Gold Mines in Kansas and Nebraska, with a Description of the Shortest and Most Direct Route from Chicago to Pike's Peak & Cherry Creek Gold Mines* (Polhemus & de Vries, New York, 1859), 3. Referred to hereafter as Polhemus, *1859 Traveler's Guide.*

[3]The offices of the Pike's Peak Express Company and of the Pony Express were located in the Patee House. Broadside (illustration), Ray A. Billington, "Books That Won the West," *The American West,* IV (August 1967), 30.

The Tremont House was a Chicago hotel. R.V. Kennedy & Co., *D. B. Cooke & Co.'s [Chicago] City Directory for the Year 1859–60* (Chicago, 1859), 504.

I saw the arrival and departure of the first express that ever passed between St. Joseph and St. [San] Francisco/[4] They made a great display on starting the express/ First the dispatches are all made up and laid on the counter then the horse is brought into the office and placed facing the officer/ The letters are placed into the saddlebags. The driver takes his seat/ The telegraph operator makes up the last dispatches from New York and Washington/ The cannon at the doors thunder the warning to the ferryboat which is in readiness to convey the messenger across the river/ And now the last minute having expired the last dispatches are placed in the bag marked with the hour and the minute of starting/ The cannon thunders out once more and before its smoke has cleared away the messenger is off swift as the best mettle of his horse can take him one mile at a headlong gallop through the city and then he gets on board the ferryboat/ In five minutes more he is in Kansas on the road for the Pacific/ This rider stays on his horse two hours and a half or while he is making twenty five miles. Then there is another horse and rider waiting. The saddlebags are changed to

[4]One unresolved problem in the calculations of the dating of Young's remarks is posed by this sentence. If Young has accounted for every day, he reached St. Joseph on April 19 after a day's ride on the railroad on his third day from Chicago. Later (see next paragraph of text below) he writes, "We stopped in St. Joseph about four days." The *first* Pony Express rider left St. Joseph on April 3 and the *first* arrived on April 13. Young was probably mistaken in thinking he had witnessed the *first* departure and arrival.

the fresh horse/ The new rider jumps into his seat
and off again once more and so on changing about
the same distance until at last they reach San Francisco in seven or eight days.[5] It was indeed a grand
idea the interchange of news across the continent in
such a short time almost equal to railroad speed the
distance being about twenty hundred miles, over
mountains and through deserts.

We stopped in St. Joseph about four days and
then concluded it was time to proceed on our long
journey. We went down to the Missouri River and
took passage on board of a ferryboat for Bellemont a
village on the Kansas side about five miles from St.
Joe.[6] The Missouri River here is about four hundred
yards wide. The water is very yellow being a mixture
of about one half part of sand and water. It has a
very rapid current running at the rate of about ten
miles an hour. In some places it is very deep but the
sand bars are all movable which makes it very dangerous to navigation. After stemming the current for
about an hour we landed at Bellemont. We found
the town to consist of about three frame houses

[5] Young's information is approximate. Each horse covered
an average of ten miles, the distance between stations. Depending on terrain, each rider went from thirty-five to seventy miles at a stint. The average time to cover the entire
route was ten days. Oscar O. Winther, *The Transportation
Frontier: Trans-Mississippi West, 1865–1890* (New York,
1964), 52–53.
[6] The "Steam Ferry to Bellemont on Kansas side runs in
connection with the trains on this road." Polhemus, *1859
Traveler's Guide,* 5.

and a tremendous high bluff raising at about an angle of forty five degrees. After an infinite deal of hard labor we succeeded in getting our horses and wagons to the top and then men and animals were so tired out that we put up our tent and were glad to find rest for the night the first night of our camping out.

Each one made himself useful providing the evening meal or attending to the horses. Some made a fire, some worked at putting up the tent and made a bed of blankets and quilts on the bare ground and others cutting ham making coffee and providing the other articles belonging to the prairie traveler's life. The supper was delicious and sharpened as our appetites were by vigorous exercise and a strange climate we enjoyed the meal hugely. Ye epicures and good livers you should come out on the prairie shove a wagon up a hill about seven hundred feet high and you could appreciate a hearty healthy meal without fearing any of the pangs of indigestion or dyspepsia. After supper we chatted a while and then turned under our blankets for a night's rest, and I must say I never rested better in my life, I slept soundly all night and woke in the morning thoroughly refreshed, Our first day and night's experience on the prairie did not have many hardships.

We turned out at the first streak of day and then had a very busy time till we got started. Some brought in the horses cleaned and harnessed them, Others pulled up our tent and packed it and the bedclothes into the wagon and others were busy preparing the breakfast. At sunrise we were all ready and started across the bluffs directly westward through the plains of Kansas. The road today lay through a very rough rolling country the hills being about two hundred feet high, no sooner on the top of one expecting then to find a good road, but instead we could look down a tremendous steep hill so very abrupt that we were compelled to chain two of the wheels of the wagon to prevent it from running into the horses. The scenery through this place was very fine, The grass was luxuriant and green on one side and boundless as the ocean. On the other lay a thick belt of timber which enclosed the Missouri River. The road was thickly strewed with immigrants far as the eye could reach over the rolling hills all rushing on eagerly bound for the same golden country.

On account of the rough nature of the roads we made only twenty miles this day and camped at sunset within a few rods of a Kansas farmer's house. We purchased from them some warm biscuits and fresh milk and had a supper fit for a king. In the evening the farmer invited us to his house, There was to be a singing school there that night. We had a very merry time of it. There was a good many young folks present, We sang some songs together and then a rivalry started between Illinois and Kansas to see which could sing the best songs and in the best style. After a few hours of merry strife we acknowledged the supremacy of the Kansas girls.

In the morning we started again on our pilgrimage not feeling so merry and cheerful on account of the previous night's enjoyment. The road still continued very rough and hard on our animals, We were still on the bluffs of the Missouri River which in this place are about twenty five miles wide. Oh the hardships of going up and down those bluffs I shall never forget. We had to double teams going up hill and then take hold of the wagons and help. Every ten yards we would block the wheels and take a breathing spell and so on resting at intervals till at last we gained the top feeling very thankful indeed and expecting at last to find the long promised level land, but bitter disappointment there lay a steep descent and on the other side another terrific hill, It was almost enough to discourage and make us give up in despair. But we hung to it with forced cheerfulness, encouraging one another and cracking jokes at the expense of those fellows who had paid from fifty to seventy five dollars for their passage or as we would tell them for the privilege of shoving a wagon up hill all day.

On this day we again made only twenty miles owing to the uneven roads. We camped at night foot sore and tired on the banks of a beautiful little stream called Walnut Creek. It was a nice camping place as there was wood water and grass plenty. I now began to enjoy in earnest the solitary expanse of prairies and the deprivation of the luxuries of cities. After traveling all day over the hot shelterless prairie it was indeed a delightful feeling of repose came over us as we saw in the far distance the long belt of timber which conceals within its green boughs the stream of cool running water. It is as unfailing a sign of water on the western prairies, as the oasis is to the parched and wearied traveler on the great African desert.

This night we enjoyed ourselves hugely, had a good meal of stewed rabbits and prairie chickens which we killed during the day, and as the evening was cold we built a rousing fire got out our buffalo skins spread them on the grass all round the fire and stretched ourselves at full length to rest our weary limbs. And now commenced the merry part of our voyage, The joke, song, and laugh went round as merrily as if it was all a holiday freak and we entirely forgot the solemn fact that there were more hills to be surmounted on the morrow, forgot all the vexations and annoyances of the day and thought only of spending pleasantly the passing hour. The night was so beautifully calm and clear that we concluded not to set our tent and we set our guard and lay down to sleep in regular Indian style by our campfire.

The night passed calmly without any annoyance from our horses or what more frequently happens from our fellow travelers, but I must say that thefts are of very rare occurrence, The infliction of immediate punishment which is the invariable rule of our society on the plains the offender being caught is instantly tried by a jury picked upon the road/ The witnesses both for and against are heard and if not proved he is discharged forthwith. If guilty he will be punished according to the enormity of the offense. If for horse or mule stealing or murder he is hung to the nearest tree. If a less grievous crime he is tied to a tree or wagon wheel and receives from ten to one hundred lashes on the bare back the amount to be fixed by the jury. The certainty of immediate and severe punishment is a wholesome check to the evil disposed so much so that of late we have not many fears of being annoyed from that source.

On the third day we commenced our journey very early as we had to make thirty miles to the next camping ground. Our old enemies the bluffs still surrounded us and made it tiresome work. About noon today some antelope came in sight and we had a very exciting time trying to shoot some of them but could not accomplish it, as they were very shy, and we were not acquainted with the manner of hunting them. We afterwards found it out from the Indians. You can take a red handkerchief tie it to your ramrod, and find a low hollow place in the prairie, raise your signal high in your hand, and let it fall quite naturally to the ground/ Keep repeating this signal every two or three minutes, and if there are any antelope within two or three miles they will run towards the signal/ You have your gun all ready and when they show their heads above the brow of the hill you can shoot them without any trouble/ If you have a double-barreled rifle you will perhaps have a chance to shoot two of them as they generally feed in pairs. The flesh of the antelope is the finest meat I ever tasted/ It is nice tender and delicious far ahead of venison.

About sundown we made Rock Creek where we encamped for the night/ This was the hardest day we yet had on the road. We were so fatigued that we would almost as soon go without any supper as to have to prepare [it]/ However we stirred ourselves up got our supper rolled up in our blankets and felt as well satisfied with our rest and refreshment as if we had the best accommodations of the Sherman House/[7] You who live in cities having all the comforts of home cannot imagine the luxurious feeling that comes upon the prairie traveler after the day's toilsome march is over and he is enjoying himself by his evening campfire. It is worth going hundreds of miles to experience the pleasures of the hunter's life even for one brief month.

The following morning we rose as fresh as larks went down to the clear stream had a good wash in its cool waters, prepared our breakfast and started again on our toilsome journey/ On this day about

[7]Chicago's Sherman House hotel. Kennedy, *Cooke City Directory of 1859-60,* 504.

noon we got to the Indian reserve about sixty square miles reserved for their use by the government.[8] At this point where the road runs through the reserve it is about thirty miles from the Missouri River/ It extends down to the river and is splendid hunting ground having noble forests plenty of game and fine streams with the best kind of fish. The Indians living in this reserve are about half civilized/ They build frame houses have corn planted, and seem to be an industrious and contented people/

As we were traveling along the road some Indians came out to meet us and asked us in to see an old man. We went with them and saw a neat frame house that they lived in and beside it a wigwam made of birchbark in which the old man lived/ They could not induce him to live in the house. In the center of the wigwam there was a campfire the smoke going out through the roof, and about twenty squaws ranged around the fire sitting on buffalo skins. The old man lay on one side on a huge pile of skins. He was the most withered looking remains of humanity I ever saw/ There was not a particle of flesh on his bones/ He was shrunk to about the size of a boy ten

[8] Young is either confused on his chronology or has received some misinformation about the precise location of this reservation. It could have involved any one of several groups. See, especially, Plate CXXXIV and the corresponding references to the "Schedule of Indian Land Cessions" to which it is keyed, in Charles C. Royce, comp., "Indian Land Cessions in the United States," *Eighteenth Annual Report of the Bureau of American Ethnology . . . 1896–97*, Part 2 (Washington, 1899), 648–949.

years old he that once according to his childrens'
story had been a powerful chief and great warrior/
His teeth were entirely gone and he was quite blind/
The Indians told us he was one hundred and twenty
one years old and [we] have not the least doubt of it/
Notwithstanding his age and infirmities he managed
to ask us for "money"/ As we went out of the wigwam we each slipped a piece of silver into his hand/
He returned his thanks by giving us a hearty shake
of his hand.

After this small interruption we resumed our
journey. We passed across several small streams/
This day we traveled about twenty five miles and
reached the town of Marysville one hundred miles
from St. Joe at nightfall.[9] We camped on the banks
of the Big Blue River which runs through the town.
It is a very nice stream having the peculiar characteristic of all Kansas rivers, viz. about one foot deep,
twenty wide and clear running water with a gravelly
bottom/ The water is cool and tastes first rate. In the
neighborhood of this river the bluffs are almost as
high as those on the shore of the Missouri.

The town has a very fine site on the bluffs commanding a view of the prairies for miles on every
side. It is a place of some importance being the last
outfitting place for immigrants for Pike's Peak, Utah
and California and the residence of the government
inspector of goods for U.S. troops in the West. The
trains are here examined to ascertain that the sup-

[9] Marysville is the seat of Marshall County, Kansas.

plies are all right and to prevent the shipment of any
contraband article at the expense of the government.
The town has a population of about one thousand
one pretty respectable looking street and some first
rate stores a newspaper office land office a few law-
yers and some doctors.

After looking all about the town we packed up and
turned again westward/ Our first job was to get
across the Big Blue a very difficult undertaking with
our heavily loaded wagon/ There is a very steep
descent of about one hundred feet to the bed of the
river in the middle a bed of quicksand and a hill to
raise on the other side however we hitched four
horses to each wagon and went at it with a will. It
was very easy to get down but we stuck fast in the
middle and the horses could not budge another
inch/ Joe and myself were standing on the feed box
and in getting down to help the horses Joe caught
his foot in a rope and dove head first into the stream/
The water was as cold as ice and the morning frosty
but there was no pity for him but all had a hearty
laugh at his expense. I was more fortunate and
jumped in without getting any wet the water not
being deep and we all wore long miners' boots/ By
dint of hard pulling and pushing we succeeded in
getting out of the ugly hole but had the same operation to repeat to bring across the other wagon.

Once more on the road the aspect of the country
changed somewhat from its uneven hilly aspect/ The
country was slightly undulating/ The grass [was] so

fine and green it was really a charming sight, The boundless prairie [was as] far as the eye could reach in every direction, I cannot compare it to anything but the ocean. We journeyed on pleasantly without incident of any kind. The weather now was getting pretty warm, It was now uncomfortably so, There was a high wind blowing, The dust rose in clouds and almost blinded us, To add to our troubles we met no water during the day's travel so that horses and men were almost exhausted. We traveled thirty mile and camped on the Big Sandy River for the night, This stream is precisely like the Big Blue River only is some smaller being about ten feet wide. We camped here for the night the most dirty fatigued looking set of gold hunters you could find on the road between St. Joe and Denver City.

In the morning we arose fresh as if we had slept on feather beds and resumed our journey, We met nothing worth describing on this day, The country had about the same appearance as on the previous day, We made twenty five miles and camped on the Little Sandy River a beautiful little stream but so small that in any other country it would be called a rivulet.

The next day about noon we struck the Little Blue River the most singular river I saw in this strange country.[10] It is about three hundred miles long about twenty broad and three deep, It runs through a level

[10]The Little Sandy River (Little Sandy Creek) is a tributary of the Big Sandy River (Big Sandy Creek) which in turn is a tributary of the Little Blue River. The last is a tributary of the Big Blue River.

prairie the water even with the surface of the ground/ The water is a very fine taste and of a deep blue color/ If you take some up in a glass it has the appearance of having been colored. There was plenty of fish swimming about which could plainly be seen through the water. We now met plenty of game: ducks jackass rabbits prairie chickens in abundance and we fared in most luxurious style. Our road lay parallel with the river and almost along its banks through the day/ I was charmed with the looks of that beautiful stream. At night we camped on its banks the prettiest camping ground we yet had. After supper we got out our flutes had some music and singing and enjoyed ourselves till a late hour of the night.

In the morning we resumed our journey/ Again all day along the banks of the Blue/ Still the same beautiful color in the water the same level prairie on either side/ At noon we came to a ranch called Pawnee Ranch/ I went in to ask some questions of the proprietor but on entering the door was struck dumb on seeing on the counter a human skull with the following inscription on the forehead "Died from asking too many questions"/ I drew back again quickly without making any inquiries of the churlish owner/ I suppose he was much annoyed from travelers and put up this hideous warning as an answer to all who passed by. We camped on the stream had our dinner and let our cattle graze for a couple of hours and then resumed our journey/

Today we met some of Majors & Russell's return trains from Camp Floyd Utah and Pike's Peak,[11] There was three separate trains of forty wagons each every one drawn by six yoke of oxen. The drivers were principally Mexicans not half as civilized looking as Indians/ Their appearance was rather singular/ Their dress was made of buckskin/ No covering of their feet or on their heads from which flowed long straight hair which lay loose about their face and shoulders/ They were very friendly each one shaking hands with us as they passed on. This afternoon we also met the Pony Express returning from San Francisco/ He passed us like the wind and we could not get a single word of news/ We camped tonight on the [Little] Blue River again.

The following day at noon we parted from this beautiful little stream having traveled fifty miles along its banks. We now struck out on the broad open prairie on the old military road to California/ This road has been well worn by travel/ It is about one hundred feet broad and cut down from constant use about one foot its whole width/ The whole immigration to and from California in 1848 and 1850 was over this highway/ It is now a splendid road the peculiar nature of the soil rendering it when exposed to the sun as hard as brick without any assistance from man/ It is far ahead of the smoothest

[11] The Russell, Majors and Waddell firm dominated freighting business on the Great Plains and in the Rockies. Winther, *Transportation Frontier*, 26.

macadamized roads in the States a wagon loaded with six ton making no impression whatever on its flinty surface.

Tonight we had to camp on the open prairie without wood or water/ The prospect was not all [at] all encouraging, and we could not help contrasting it with our abundance of the night previous of the Little Blue. We pitched our tent and camped on the side of the road/ Picketed our horses and downhearted and unhappy we threw ourselves on our blankets to find some rest. This was the first time I began to think of home with many regrets for leaving it/ All the hardships and difficulties of our undertaking then rose before my mind vividly and I could not help thinking we had sacrificed our good established business the comforts of home and friends to come on this wild goose chase for now in its sober reality I could not consider it in any other light. So curious is it that no sooner do we realize a small share of hardship than we commence to complain of what we brought upon ourselves knowing and expecting even worse than what we then experienced.

The next morning we commenced our journey again/ About noon we came to a pool of dirty water/ We camped here for dinner refreshed ourselves and started again on our journey/ That night we camped within ten miles of the Platte River but had to spend another night without wood or water/ We however felt more cheerful tonight at the near prospect of relief.

In the morning we rose very early and were again upon the road/ In about three hours we struck the great Platte River at Grand Island ten miles below Fort Kearney/ We were so starved out for want of cooked victuals that we determined to spend the remainder of the day and night here.

The river at this place is about a mile wide having a large green island in the center. The water will average about one foot in depth all the way across/ It is however very hard for man or horse to cross on account of quicksand/ Indeed you may say the river is nothing more than a moving bed of sand/ You could not drink it unless you were almost famished with thirst. We could not use it until it lay in a vessel for an hour to settle. On the banks of the river there was a thick belt of cottonwood timber about one eighth mile thick/ Our camp was in this wood/ Shortly after encamping as we were standing on the edge of the river we saw some huge animal moving on the island/ We soon found that it was a buffalo/ Joe and Jim[12] took hold of their guns jumped into the river and waded across to the island but they could not get within [range] of him/ It is almost impossible to shoot a single buffalo/ They are so cautious.

We feasted gloriously today on baked bread stewed rabbit and plenty of tea and coffee/ We made

[12]This and a previous mention of "Joe" are the only times in his entire account that Young refers to any members of his party by name. Joe is probably Joseph Mullen and Jim is undoubtedly Young's brother James.

up for the privations of the three previous days. We also cooked a supply for the road so that we would have no delay but proceed on our journey/ At night we had another jolly time of it music singing and shouting with very excess of happiness.

In the morning we started again on our journey/ Our road now lay on the Platte River bottoms clear to the Rocky Mountains/ It was a perfect level till about a mile and sometimes two or three miles from the river/ Then commenced the bluffs but they never came as close to the river as our road.

We now came in sight of Fort Kearney and could see the glorious old "Star Spangled Banner" floating proudly on the breeze. The fort consists of about twenty houses occupied as barracks officers quarters and a post office enclosing a square of about one acre with twelve six pounder guns mounted three on each side of the square/ What they were placed there for I could not imagine as they could not fire them off without knocking down the buildings. It is very curious why they selected such a position for a fort/ It has no natural advantages whatever/ There is not any shelter from an enemy no elevation to the ground and it is a mile away from the river and they have not even got a mud enclosure around it and I should think in case of assault the insiders would have no advantage over the besiegers.

We were not allowed to stop in the immediate neighborhood of the "fort" the rules being strict that no one should camp within two miles. I stayed behind to get letters/ I found some from home the first I received since leaving/ We were as eager to get news from home as if we had been away years instead of only two weeks. I read my letters found all well at home and then went out to the square to see the drill/ There was two companies United States Regulars fine appearing men but sadly deficient of clothing/ Almost every man was out at the knees or elbows/ Even the officers looked shabby/ I saw them trying to get gloves on which required a great deal of skill/ They were full of holes and the fingers would not go out in the right place. However badly dressed they were they understood their drill perfectly/ They were put through infantry and then another company through artillery drill.

After the drill was over we started again on our journey leaving the last outpost of civilization behind us. The weather was now commencing to get very warm/ It was on the 5th of May we passed through Kearney/ I forgot to mention that at the other side of the [river from] the fort there is quite a town called Kearney City/ It has about thirty houses and a population of perhaps one hundred/ I suppose the way the inhabitants support themselves is by selling vegetables milk butter &c. to the soldiers.

The road now lay along the bank of the river sometimes close by the edge of the water and again a mile away from it. The antelope now came within range frequently and we succeeded in killing a few of them/ We now lived like princes plenty of the best kind of game with bread, butter, beans, pork salt dried apples fish tea and coffee and plenty of wood and water. We felt in such high spirits that a day's journey of thirty miles did not tire us in the least.

We were now in the Indian country and in the evening they would come round our encampment in swarms asking for food. The poor wretches were really starving, They had a long severe winter and as is usually the case failed to lay up anything, I have seen them eat a horse that dropped dead on the road. We always gave them the remains of our meals but it only made them clamorous for more, Of course we could not satisfy them, Our two wagon loads of provisions if shared among them would not make one meal for the multitudes that surround us at every meal and it was the most painful thing I ever experienced to see them watch us as we put the bite to our mouths with a most hungry entreating look. I had almost go without food as to eat in their presence but we could not get away from them, As soon as victuals were brought out they came round us in swarms.

Our journey was now very monotonous, For the ensuing four days we passed through the Pawnee and Potawatomi nations of Indians, The latter are the lowest and most degraded specimens of humanity that I yet encountered, They are almost naked live like animals and entirely devoid of morality. I have seen them eat a horse that died from hardship and starvation/ They would tear it with their teeth as ravenously as a pack of wolves.

Our guide book now informed us that we had one hundred miles before us without wood of any kind/ We were obliged to carry a supply with us/ We chopped down a cottonwood tree took off a log and tied it under our wagons before we started/ We cooked and laid in what we considered a good supply for three days so that we would not have to use our wood unless for making coffee.

All things being prepared we started out on this dreary looking desert. In most places it was devoid of grass and what was very strange not a sign of a shrub tree or even a willow the peculiar characteristic of this country being to have timber on its river banks and in no other place. Our horses suffered severely here/ They had no grass and had to subsist entirely on corn which made them very weak and we were compelled thereby to make very short journeys. We made the hundred miles in five days and then felt rejoiced thinking we were out of the desert but there were no indications of such a happy change/

We journeyed on day after day for ten days/ Still the same dreary waste/ Nothing to see but river prairie and sky and the sufferings and hardships we endured during that time will remain impressed on my mind forever. Our horses were almost dying from starvation. Ourselves had nothing to eat but raw ham and half baked cornmeal warmed by a few buffalo chips which we found on the prairie but they would not make a strong enough fire to thoroughly cook it/ No tea or coffee during the whole time/ The gnawings of our stomach combined with the anxiety and trouble of daily disappointments made us almost walking skeletons.

So that the first "land" as we called it that we made O'Fallon's Bluffs[13] was so joyful a sight to us that we set up a loud and long shout and such was our eagerness to reach it that only for our weakened state we would have run towards it. Indeed I believe that if a mile of fabulous richness lay behind us we would not stop a moment to pick up its golden treasures. In the evening we camped once more under the grateful shelter of the cottonwoods/ That night we had a most glorious feast/ We had stewed rabbit fried ham baked bread and good hot tea/ It looked to our empty stomachs to be a feast good enough for prince or king to enjoy. After our supper we looked up good quarters for our poor starved horses. We found a place where the grass was splen-

---

[13]The bluffs were on the south side of the South Platte River opposite the present town of O'Fallons. "At O'Fallon's bluffs is a mail station and one other trading-house, with plenty of goods of all kinds." Luke Tierney, *History of the Gold Discoveries on the South Platte River* (Pacific City, Iowa, 1859), 26. This guide book is reprinted in LeRoy R. Hafen, ed., *Pike's Peak Gold Rush Guidebooks of 1859* (Glendale, California, 1941).

did and tied them there for the night leaving a watch
to look out for their safety, We then lay down and
had a comfortable night's sleep.

The place where we encamped was called "Fremont's Orchard" on account of the great "Pathfinder" stopping a night there while on his journey
to the Pacific.[14] It might with justness be called an
orchard, In the center was an open space of about
ten acres, All around it were rows of wild apple tree
commonly called "crab" growing as regularly and
even distances apart as if planted by the hand of
man, Indeed I never saw straighter rows of trees in
the best kept gardens of our city. It was a most
singular freak of nature. We stopped in this beautiful place the following day to refresh ourselves and
recruit our horses, If time permitted I would like to
stop there a month.

We were now 580 miles from St. Joe and according to the guide book had only one hundred miles
more to Denver City but on account of its deceiving

[14]Taking Young's itinerary sequence of O'Fallon's Bluffs,
Fremont's Orchard, forks of the Platte, and the cutoff road,
Fremont's Orchard is simply out of place here. Fremont's
Orchard was still further along the South Platte River, east of
present Orchard and south of Goodrich in western Morgan
County, Colorado, beyond the cutoff road where his party
left the old trail. Also, in all probability, he was confused on
his identification. He describes the trees as "wild apple" or
"crab." Fremont's Orchard was composed of cottonwood.
LeRoy R. Hafen, ed., *Overland Routes to the Gold Fields, 1859,
from Contemporary Diaries* (Glendale, California, 1942), 155
and note.

us so many times we could put no more confidence
in its lying descriptions.[15]

We now resumed our journey again along the
banks of the river as before the country having the
same appearance of river on one side bluffs on the
other and the level bottoms on which lay our road/
At this place is the Forks of the Platte River/[16] The
way I first perceived it was from the sudden narrow-
ing of the river/ It was about two miles wide and all
at once it became as [a] small stream about two hundred yards wide/ At first I thought it was only a
large island but as we traveled along for miles I concluded it must be the "Forks." Our course lay along
the South Fork until the next day at noon when we
came to a place where they had made a new road
a short cut to Denver but which we were prejudiced
against from accounts heard on the road and also
from a letter received from a friend in Denver.

We stopped at the "cutoff" for dinner and I
thought from talking it over so often that there was
no doubt but that we would keep the "old road"/

[15]While it is not possible to determine which guide book
Young was using, and while exaggeration and unreliability
frequently misled those who relied too heavily on guide
books, Young himself was apparently confused as to his present location. This may be explained, in part, by the possibility that the present account was written after his return to
Chicago, perhaps from notes taken while on the trip. See Billington, "Books That Won the West." See also previous note.

[16]The North Platte and the South Platte rivers converge
into the Platte River near the present city of North Platte,
Nebraska.

There was a vote taken upon it and to my intense surprise the vote was unanimous for the new road with the exception of myself. I told them the disadvantages and probable dangers from hostile Indians want of water and grass and fuel from being deprived of which we suffered so much recently. All would not do, The runner employed by the road told them it was twenty miles shorter and that they thought would make up for all dangers and difficulties.[17] So I had to submit but under protest and we started on our journey.

Our numbers were now about fifty good strong able bodied men. We determined to stick closely together and keep a strict watch on all sides for

[17] One guide book explained that the cutoff had been explored during the previous winter on an "air-line" from Denver to the mouth of Beaver Creek. It saved emigrants "some fifty miles," and spared them "almost impassable stretches of deep sand." Better still it promised "grass, wood, some timber and plenty of antelopes." Henry Villard, *The Past and Present of the Pike's Peak Gold Regions* (St. Louis, 1860. Reprinted by LeRoy Hafen, ed., Princeton, 1932), 169.

By no means did travelers agree on the desirability of the cutoff. Controversy raged in the Denver newspapers on the subject. A "Pike's Peak Humbug!!!" testimonial of over twenty emigrants that warned that the road was "full NINETY MILES LONG, SANDY, Minus Water, save what is alkalied, and is in fact, a nuisance and a humbug!" appeared for several weeks in the pages of the Denver *Weekly Bulletin* (May 2, 9, 16, 30, 1860) and the *Rocky Mountain News* (May 2, 16, 23, 1860). This was denounced in a letter in the *Bulletin* (May 23, 1860) as "false, malicious and slanderous." Those who made such false reports "claim, but should no longer have the title of gentlemen." Several "certificates" which extolled the virtues of the cutoff followed the letter.

Indians. We were now in the Cheyenne country a vindictive hostile and numerous tribe. Our journey was quiet and without alarm of any kind this afternoon/ We camped at evening on a small rivulet called Beaver Creek/ The water was about one inch deep and six inches wide but quite clear and cool. There was also plenty of wood, and a little grass for our animals/ We were all nice and comfortable but for the fear of Indians/ We determined to have half our party stay on guard during the night. It was my watch for the early part of the night/ The night being cold we built a rousing fire and chatted and told yarns without being disturbed in the least/ At twelve we called up the other watch went to rest and slept quietly till morning.

We then got up cooked breakfast and once more plunged into the Cheyenne country/ About two hours after starting we noticed a single Indian on the right hand side of the road about half a mile distant/ At first we did not think any thing of the occurrence but in a short time we found out from his actions that he was a spy probably sent during the night to our camp to ascertain our numbers but on account of making a circle of our wagons which we usually did in a hostile country, he was unable to see our tents or count us in any way so he waited till we got on the road when he could easily do so. We saw him at intervals of about fifteen minutes for about an hour and then he disappeared and for two hours more we could not see a single trace of an

Indian. Then it being about noon we camped to provide our dinner,

We made a large circle of our wagons "lariated" our horses and commenced busily to prepare our dinner being in the inside of the wagons. On account of not seeing any signs of Indians we grew careless, and did not set any guard, We had our dinner cooked and were sitting down on the grass to enjoy it comfortably when all at once like an electric shock came the alarming cry of Indians, Every man jumped instantly to his feet grasped his rifle and pistols and as we looked out between the wagons we saw multitudes of warriors pouring down towards us fast as their horses could gallop from all directions, It seemed as if the very hills sprang suddenly to life.

On they came rushing at a gallop up to our very wagons, We then presented our rifles and they suddenly wheeled and turned away out of range of our bullets, There they stood deliberating whether they should make an attack and there we stood fifty men opposed to more than a thousand of those wild devils the "Comanche" of Kansas, I seen some very white faces among our party but the set teeth and firm grasp on the rifle showed that it was not from cowardice as every man was resolved to fight desperately and before he would lose his scalp to stop the howlings of five or six of the infernal hounds.

Each party maintained their position for about two hours without any hostile demonstration from the Indians/ We then considered that they would besiege us till night and as we had no defenses they could fall upon us with every advantage in their favor. This would not suit us at all/ If we had to fight we would rather have it come in daylight when we could have the advantage of position. We felt that something must be done and done soon or we should be hemmed in without hope of escape/ It would be the height of madness to remain in our present position so we resolved to leave it or provoke the Indians to immediate attack, so ten of our number brought in our horses harnessed them up to the wagons and made all ready for a start/ The other forty still kept the rifle on the cock and presented at the foe. We took a vote on the question whether we should remain in our present position with the certainty of being attacked as soon as night set in or to travel on trusting to fortune to lead us to some place where we could have some chance to defend ourselves/

The vote was unanimous for starting as it could not make our danger more at all events. So our wagons formed in line on the road and we divided ourselves half marching on each side of the wagons with our rifle in hand and pistols and knives in hand ready for action. The Indians now pressed very closely on to us sometimes so close that we should present our guns at them when they would go off again to a considerable distance/ They tried to throw us off our guard by pretending that they were not on the "warpath" and offering to trade moccasins buffalo robes and buckskins but we were not to be caught by their wily stratagem/ Whenever they approached too near we pointed our guns at them when they scampered off like a lot of frightened sheep. They are the most cowardly wretches in existence/ To think that over one thousand of them well armed stout men were afraid of fifty white men/

Things continued in the same shape for the next two hours the Indians following us but keeping a respectable distance away/ Sometimes they would meet together in a large group as if consulting together then they would rush towards us with whoops and yells and we would expect that our hour had come/ They made this feint two or three times/ It was another dodge to throw us off our guard and if they found us unprepared make a real attack of it.

We now felt the most gloomy apprehension/ It was within two hours of sundown and we were afraid they would follow us till night and we resolved to make a charge on them fire a volley and either drive them off or bring on an engagement/ Just as we were ready to do this they gave two or three yells and rushed over the bluffs and out of our sight/ In five minutes there was not an Indian to be seen/ Still we did not relax a bit of our discipline as we believed this was another dodge of the cunning rascals to throw us off our guard however we did not see them again and we came to a hill at dusk and as it was well adapted for defense we determined to camp on it for the night. We drew our wagons into a circle having our tents and horses in the inside and there was plenty of timber for shelter, We felt secure for the night.

This was a most harassing day on us all having no dinner and traveled thirty miles and the continual alarm and excitements of the day almost prostrated us with weakness, We got some supper and set a guard and then turned in to get some rest and I am sure each one before lying down this night returned thanks to God for having preserved us through so many dangers through the day.

We still had many apprehensions for the night, The guards were very vigilant and gave two false alarms, Each time we sprang to our feet grasped our arms expecting that the enemy were upon us. But happily the night passed without any appearance of Indians nor did we ever afterwards see anything of the tribe.

I am sure they traveled ahead of us in the evening when they left us and were in ambush probably very close to us, but finding us on our guard they were too cowardly to attack us. They are such wretched cowards that they will never make an attack openly on any armed party no matter how greatly they outnumber them but they will skulk round till they can take you unprepared and then woe to the unlucky immigrant that falls into their blood thirsty hands, They were never known to show mercy. Our escape from them was providential for we afterwards found out that they were in a state of starvation and rendered desperate by hunger/ It is a wonder they did not attack us. They would do so but our determined position and the knowledge that we were well armed and would fight desperately kept them in check.

On the following morning we resumed our journey/ Suffered some this day from the want of water and the sandy roads. I think by this time the company wished we had taken the old and well known road along the Platte River/ In the afternoon of this day we met some Arapaho Indians/ We were now in their country/ They appeared to be very friendly and we traded some with them/ I purchased a buffalo skin from one of them for a pint cup of sugar/ It was a splendid hide full size and worth ten dollars in Chicago.

Tonight we camped within thirty miles of Denver City and according to our calculations of distance 750 miles from St. Joe. When we camped in the evening several of the Indians came round our camp for the purpose of trading/ After awhile some of our party started some games of activity and strength to see if the Indians could beat us but in every feat the white man excelled except in the single one of on horseback. Running, jumping, shooting with the rifle and in throwing weight the white man was superior. But the Indian could perform some astonishing feats on horseback/ One was riding on one side of his horse so that we who were standing one hundred yards distant could not say whether he was on the horse's back or not. Another one was laying three stones down on the road about twenty yards apart and then the Indian would gallop towards them pick up one stone sit erect on his horse again turn over on the side of his horse just holding on by one toe and one hand pick up the second one and so on with the third all done in an instant. So fast that the eye could scarcely follow his movements he rode in triumphantly with the three stones in his hands. These Indians appeared to be very friendly and well disposed towards us eager to trade skins and moccasins for anything we might offer them.

We camped this night on a prairie dog city about ten miles square, They are a queer looking little animal about the size of a cat fat and plump looking. They are very numerous, All that great extent of ground is full of holes about one yard apart. It is very hard to kill one of those little creatures, They are very shy and at the first appearance of an enemy in their vicinity their heels twinkle in the air and they disappear in their holes in an instant. Then commences a deafening chorus of voices all barking furiously. It is very hard to get a shot at one of them and if you succeed in killing it the others will pull it into the hole before you can lay hold of it, We used to count it a great feat to capture one of them, It was only for the sport as the flesh is unfit to eat. The most remarkable thing about these little things is the mixture of races in their family the dog, the owl and the rattlesnake all living peacefully in the same hole/ I have seen them all go down together many hundred times/ I think it is a very strange freak of nature.

In this part of the country were a great many rabbits called here jackass rabbits but I am told by people that are well informed on the matter that they are the regular old country hare/ They are very large/ We succeeded in killing some and the flesh was excellent. There is a knack in hunting them which if you do not know you could not kill one in a month/ When one starts up before you you must stand still and then he will stand still also and sit on his hind legs and face right towards you/ If he is too far off for a shot advance slowly towards him in a straight line/ If you go zigzag he will know it at once and start off/ In this way you can come close enough to shoot him/ If he does take the alarm and start stop still again and he will not go far until he stops when you can repeat the same maneuver again/ I would never miss killing one that I started unless he might happen to get to his burrow.

The next day we resumed our journey traveling through the prairie dog city about ten miles/ That day I saw millions of them/ It is a wonder to me how they manage to live/ There is no grass growing on the place/ It is so cut up and trampled by them. The road today was very heavy and sandy and we found no water for twenty miles/ We then came to a nice stream running from the mountains called Clear Creek and we camped for the night on its banks.

They have discovered coal in this place/ There was a few men to work taking it out for to supply Denver City/[18] The first evidences of civilization we had seen for fifteen days since we left Fort Kearney about five hundred miles.

The Rocky Mountains now loomed grandly before our eyes/ Every thing on the sides of the mountains could be plainly seen and I could not believe that we were more than five miles distant from them. This was the eighth day they were in sight/ We first saw them one hundred and sixty miles from here/ We got the first glimpse of them in the afternoon two hours before sunset/ The day was remarkably bright and clear and we saw what we at first supposed to be a cloud straight before us to the west/ After looking for a few minutes I noticed that it did not alter its position in the least and if it was a cloud it must drift in some direction. Its appearance was pyramidal and of a bright blue color/ After watching it about an hour I became convinced that it was the mountains and I afterwards found out that it was Long's Peak about two hundred and fifty miles distant said to be the highest peak of the Rocky Mountains. The next day it was plainly in sight as we traveled towards it. It appeared to raise out of the earth just as a ship raises out of the water at sea. On the third day we could distinguish the snow line distinctly. On the fourth day Pike's Peak with

[18]This may be a case of mistaken identification. What creek he referred to remains evasive.

its sugar loaf head rose into sight. On the fifth day the whole mountain range rose out of the plains just like a ship covered by the waves and suddenly emerging into sight.

It was truly a grand looking sight and one that I can never forget, There was something terribly grand in those tremendous rocks covered with eternal snow, I felt so elevated at the sight that I considered that I was already well repaid for all the trials and hardships I endured in coming here, On the sixth and seventh day they continued to raise showing new beauties of landscape every moment till on the eighth morning when just as the sun rose we stood apparently at their very base and it seemed as if they were hanging over us though still twenty five miles distant.

Chapter II

The Urban Frontier:
Denver, 1860

AFTER viewing the mountains for about an hour we took our line of march again although it was Sunday morning for Denver City [was] only ten miles distant, We were now approaching the Platte River again, The city is situated on its banks and we had some pretty rough bluffs to climb. At about noon we climbed an unusually high one and as we reached its summit Denver City lay stretched before us at our feet. It was a novel looking sight to us weary and almost exhausted prairie travelers, I could hardly believe my eyes, The goal of all our desires reached at last, There it lay a gem on the sides of the largest mountains in the world. The city made a very fine appearance, The streets were broad and regular and crossed at right angles, The town site was very level being on the Platte River bottoms and the river winding like a silver thread through its very center and then the eye could trace it to the very foot of the mountain, The houses were mostly built of wood and had a singular appearance, They were new nearly all of them built the preceding summer and they had never been painted. We descended the bluff about two hundred feet high and camped once more on the Platte River.

Denver City has a most beautiful site/ Through its center runs a splendid looking river/ It is perfectly level/ On the east side stretches the boundless prairies that we had traversed/ On the west loomed up the majestic Rocky Mountains seemingly overhanging the city although distant fifteen miles. Long's Peak their highest summit stood like a giant sentinel directly in front of the city its lofty peak covered with eternal snow/ Pike's Peak to the southwest [was] out on the prairie away from the mountains standing like some huge giant guarding the entrance of such countless wealth. Every thing was as distinct to our view from the city as if we were standing on them/

Although I was told on good authority that the mountains were fifteen miles distant still I could not believe it/ My opinion was that we were on its very base. We could see green trees dotting its sides for a great distance up to where all vegetation ceased then the hard gray rock seemingly as far more and then the snow line covered with white from there to its summit/ That grand old pile was a most sublime looking sight and I longed for the time when I might explore its hidden mysteries. However it was necessary to remain for a few days to recruit our horses before taking them into the mountains and also to make inquiries as to the route we should take to get there and we occupied our spare time in looking round the city.

There was some very fine buildings among which the most prominent were Major & Russell's wholesale store larger than any in Chicago, Mings Denver Hall a large brick building occupied in the lower part by a clothing store. Clark & Rugers Bank, and Forrests' Bank formerly of Chicago, the upper part was used as a billiard hall almost equal to Brunswick's in size and appointments,[19] They had five first class tables splendid lounges and arm chairs all round the room large chandeliers hanging from the ceiling and plenty of the fancy employed at the tables.

[19] Editorial interpretation of Young's erratic punctuation in this paragraph is difficult because today's business locations in 1860 Denver might not be tomorrow's. Probably this and the previous sentence should read: "Mings Denver Hall a large brick building occupied in the lower part by a clothing store, Clark & Rugers Bank, and Forrests' Bank formerly of Chicago. The upper part . . ."

The *Rocky Mountain News*, May 23, 1860, reported the recent opening "of the great 'International' of J[ohn] H. Ming, on Ferry street. This splendid hall, has not an equal west of St. Louis, and is no doubt destined to be a favorite place of resort for all lovers of innocent amusement. Billiards are the only game played. Five of Phelan's celebrated marble top tables are set up, and one or two more will soon be added."

Clark & Rugers [Gruber] Bank was Clark, Gruber & Company whose banking house also did assay work and minting. The Forrest Brothers & Company bank advertised itself as a Chicago and Denver outfit with New York, Cincinnati, St. Louis, and Milwaukee connections. The Brunswick, Monroe and Company "billiard saloon" was located in the Mechanic's Institute Hall in Chicago. Alonzo E. Ellsworth, "Early Denver Business," in Harold H. Dunham, ed., *1950 Brand Book* (Denver, 1951), 246; Robert L. Perkin, *The First Hundred Years: An Informal History of Denver and the Rocky Mountain News* (New York, 1959), 160–161; *Rocky Mountain News*, May 23, and July 4, 1860; Kennedy, *Cooke City Directory of 1859–60*, 469, 470.

From there we passed along down Blake St. a fine broad st[reet] being well and substantially built for a mile in length/ The theater a large wooden building is on this street/ Down about half its length we came to Larimer St. the place where we expected to find our friend William Clancy/ We came to his office about a square from Blake St. but were disappointed in not finding him at home. We wrote to him from Kearney but he did not expect us for a week yet and so had made a trip to the mountains expecting to be back before we arrived/ We found his partner at home Mr. Collier of Leavenworth a lawyer the business they were engaged in being legal and land transactions/[20] They had quite a number of desirable "city lots" to sell and a real estate bulletin outside the door after the fashion of our real estate offices at home. The office was quite a snug affair a well built two story wooden house very handsomely painted and grained in front/ When it was built just one year before it was called the handsomest thing of the kind in the Far West/ Its furniture was the theme of gossip on the newspaper in Denver and copied as news by the papers of the East. It is built on piles over "Cherry Creek." The time it was built there was a great body of water

[20] William Clancy and Don. C. Collier, were "Real Estate Brokers, Dealers in Farming and Mining Claims, General Agents and conveyancers." They welcomed "collecting and other legal business." *Rocky Mountain News*, May 23, 1860; J. E. Wharton, *History of the City of Denver from Its Earliest Settlement to the Present Time* (Denver, 1866), 59.

there and running very rapidly, Shortly after it was
built the creek suddenly disappeared not a remarkable thing in the neighborhood of the mountains
and kept running under its bed through the sand,
Even at this day six months after its disappearance
I found on digging a foot that the water was running and could tell the way of the current.

Mr. Collier was very kind and courteous, Offered
to assist and give us all the information in his power,
He proposed to take us round to have a view of the
city, Straight across the street from his office there
was a large brick building being put up, He informed us that it was to be a U.S. mint and post office. That put us in mind that we should get some
letters from home so he agreed to go and show us
the P.O. We passed along a few squares saw some
nice stores and came to Bradford's Corner an immense large building in which the P.O. was tempo-
rarily located,[21] The sidewalks in front were thronged

[21] Major Robert B. Bradford, merchant and freighter,
owned a "pretentious" building described as "fifty by sixty
and three stories high, the largest building of its character yet
reared in Denver." A grander scale Bradford building was under
construction in the summer of 1860, projected to be "fire proof
twenty five feet front and one hundred and twenty-five deep
. . . [and] fourteen stories high." To this description, a newspaper editor said simply, "We don't believe it." Letter, Nov-
ember 23, 1859, Libeus Barney, *Letters of the Pike's Peak Gold
Rush* (San Jose, California, 1959), 53; Stanley W. Zamonski
and Teddy Keller, *The Fifty-Niners: A Denver Diary* (Denver,
1961), 28; Raymond W. Settle, "Robert B. Bradford, Pioneer
Denver Merchant," in Erl H. Ellis, ed., *1954 Brand Book*
(Boulder, 1955), 49–64; *Rocky Mountain News*, July 4, 1860.

with people eagerly looking for news from home, I got in the string about one hundred back and had to wait patiently for my turn, It came at last and I found three letters from home, I had to pay twenty five cents postage on each that went to the express company, They carry the mail from Kearney which is as far west as the government carries it.

Just as I was emerging from the crowd and found my friend Collier I heard an altercation in a saloon across the street, There was only a few words when I heard the simultaneous report of two pistols. I got very much excited and was rushing to see what was the difficulty when my friend Collier caught me by the shoulder and very coolly told me I must not go near them, I asked him what it was and he said he guessed it was only a man shot and that we had better get out of the way as very probably there would be more shooting. I asked him with astonishment if that was the way they done things here, He said that was nothing unusual that scarcely a day passed without a murder being committed, I asked him if there was no punishment for crimes there, He said yes and that they would probably hang that fellow that killed the other just now,

We found on inquiring that was an affray between two gamblers and that one of them was dead. Mr. Collier said that if it was between two decent men that the fight occurred and they drew on each other and one fell that the survivor would not be interfered with, but public opinion was very strongly

Bradford's Corner

Contemporary sketch by J. E. Dillingham.
Lithograph by W. H. Pease and Co., Philadelphia

"Rocky Mountain News" Office, Denver, 1860

opposed to gamblers/ They were sure to be punished if caught in the least unlawful act. He asked
me to be present tonight at the trial by Lynch Law
of the murderer/ It was to take place at seven in the
evening at Denver Hall and the citizens were invited to be present by large posters stuck on the
streets. Mr. Collier formed one of the court/ He was
prosecuting attorney elected by the people/ I must
say that the court there with the exception of having
the sanction of the government is legitimate/ The
officers being regularly elected by the people they
are sworn to do justice to all men.

We strolled some further round the city went
down and called upon the editor of the Rocky Mountain News one of the daily papers published here
and had him register our names under the head of
late arrivals from the States. We purchased six copies of his paper at ten cents a copy to send home to
our friends/ We chatted pleasantly with him for an
hour or so giving him all the latest news from the
States. We then strolled round and visited some of
their hotels/ They looked very fine for such a remote place/ Some of them were well furnished and
spread good tables/ At the Pacific Hotel we had sup-
per/ After that we went out again in the street to
pass the time till the trial was to come off. One thing
was very odd looking to me/ Although the street
was crowded with people there was not a lady to be
seen/ At this time I suppose there was not a dozen
of them in the city/ I never saw one on the street

during four days that I stopped there and it looked very odd indeed.[22]

It was now near the time fixed for the trial so we went to Denver Hall and found a large crowd already assembled/ There was a great deal of loud talking and the general tenor of it bade no good to the prisoner/ In a short time after I got in the hall was crowded to its utmost capacity. There was about one thousand persons present. The judge and court now came in by a back entrance and took their seats on a raised platform/ The crier called the people to order/ Then the judge ordered the prisoner to be

[22]The Chicago *Press and Tribune*, April 12, 1860, published a letter over the signature of "Rocky Mountain," related to Young's comment: "We have a goodly number of ladies such as they are out here at Pike's Peak, but we want you to try and send us out many more. Let those handsome, agreeable Chicago belles of yours make a trip out here and select themselves, on sight, rich and good looking Pike's Peakers' husbands."

This aroused the editor of the *Rocky Mountain Herald* to reply in nearly a full page length column in his newspaper on May 5, 1860. In part, he said, "A goodly number of '*ladies such as they are!*' We would ask the people of Denver if the wives and daughters of our most respectable citizens, or if the virtuous wives and daughters of any of our citizens are to be thus ruthlessly slandered and insulted?"

Three weeks later, in the issue of May 26, 1860, the same editor happily reported that "Every day we have the pleasure of witnessing large additions made to our city in the way of families. Today we observed six teams in company from Kansas, pass our office with a lady in each, and some children attached. This looks like building up this country in a permanent style. Come on ladies, you can find society as refined here as in any part of the west."

brought forward/ He was confined in a room opening from the hall. All eyes were turned towards the
door and the prisoner was seen advancing between
two officers/ He was a young well dressed man tall
and good looking. His face was as pale as death and
his eyes were fixed and staring wildly over that vast
throng looking to find some gleam of compassion
some hope of escape but there was no such signs
among that crowd/ A low savage murmer spread
across the hall and as he heard it he knew it was
his death warrant and he fell fainting into a seat.

The trial now commenced/ The judge ordered
the sheriff to impanel a jury of twenty four men/ He
passed among the crowd and selected them in a few
minutes any man being qualified to act as juryman/
They advanced to the bar were sworn to do justice
according to the testimony between the prisoner
and the people. They then took their seats along
side and facing the prisoner. The prosecuting attorney now stood up and presented his case to the
jury/ He dwelt very hard on the prisoner's character of a gambler and the slight estimation in all of
his profession valued a human life/ He also said that
all he wanted to prove was the killing and then he
would leave it to the jury to say whether or not he
was guilty of murder.

The attorney for the defendant now made a few
remarks/ He said the customs of the country in
which we are living allowed a man to resent an
insult by taking personal satisfaction out of the

insulter and if it resulted in the death of one of the parties the survivor would not be molested. All he asked for his client was to throw away all prejudices as to his occupation and give him the same rights and privileges as the rest of his fellow citizens. He could prove to the satisfaction of the jury that the deceased had wronged and grossly insulted his client that he was only going to take a manly satisfaction out of him/ When he drew a pistol on him he was expecting this and was prepared for it/ He also drew his pistol a few shots were exchanged my client escaped unhurt/ His antagonist was shot dead.

The witnesses were now called and examined by the attorney for the people. The first witness was present at the whole affray/ He was sworn and stated that the deceased was in the saloon drinking when the prisoner came in and asked him if he would retract the lying statements he had made about him/ While asking him this question he kept his hand in his breast and stood in a threatening attitude/ The deceased answered no that he would not and put his hand in his breast to get his pistol/ As he did so and before he got it out the prisoner jerked out his pistol a revolver and fired two charges into him one of which took effect/ In his arm he now had his pistol and they exchanged a few shots one of which struck the deceased in the head killing him instantly. Three or four more witnesses were now called up/ All of them gave nearly the same testimony as to the commencement of the difficulty but some of them were of the opinion that the first shot was exchanged simultaneously, The first witness was the most positive and said that the prisoner fired the first two shots.

The attorney for the defense first and then the attorney for the prosecution each made a short speech about the same substance as the opening address, and were followed in a short summing up speech by the judge. He said that if the jury believed that the deceased had drew and fired the first shot they should acquit the prisoner but if they believed the prisoner came there with the determination of picking a quarrel and fired the first shot that they must find a verdict of guilty.

The case was now given to the jury who retired for about fifteen minutes and then returned and said they had found their verdict, The foreman came forward handed a small piece of paper to the clerk with the single word written on it "guilty", The roll was then called, Each juryman pronounced separately the verdict guilty and then were discharged. The judge now arose and asked the prisoner if he had any remarks to make why sentence should not be pronounced upon him, He simply said "nothing", The judge then addressed the people telling them that the jury had found the prisoner guilty of murder and asked them what punishment they should give him, Then arose one loud fierce yell "Hang him, hang him."

The court then asked if there was any one

opposed to this verdict of the people and a dead silence reigned for a moment broken by a yell from the prisoner so wild so terrible as almost to freeze one's heart's blood. Not a single voice to speak for the doomed one all hope left him and he fell insensible on the floor. He had some friends there the gamblers of the city but they dared not raise their voices in his favor. The reason the judge would not pronounce sentence was if he did so he would be held responsible before the law if he was ever caught in the States and could be tried for murder but by the people pronouncing his sentence no one was personally responsible. The judge now said "Let the will of the people be done" and adjourned the court,

The crowd left the hall quietly and dispersed to their homes, The whole trial only occupied three hours. In the morning at sunrise the will of the people was done and the ill fated man was executed, He said on the gallows that he did not consider himself guilty of murder before the sight of God but during his lifetime he had committed crimes which deserved the punishment he was now incurring, He was attended by a minister and died truly penitent. After he was dead they put him into a rough board coffin and buried him under the gallows.

This our second day in Denver City was spent like the other in wandering about the city, In the evening Mr. Collier agreed to show us the gambling establishments of the city, He said that we should not think that because they were so hard on the gambler that the community discountenanced gambling/ On the contrary he said that it was the most extensive business carried on there and participated in by all classes of citizens/ It was only against the blackleg or professional gambler they felt such antipathy. So in the evening we called upon him and he accompanied [us]/

On our tour we first visited an establishment on Blake St. As we entered I was astonished at the immense size of the hall and the great throng of people in it. The place was brilliantly lighted. Gold was piled in glittering heaps upon numerous tables the banker behind them busy turning the wheel of fortune or dealing the cards/ All kinds of games of chance were going on/ The crowd were betting eagerly and pressed so close upon the tables that I could scarcely see the proceedings. I watched the game earnestly/

At one table the banker was having a run of bad luck/ Every time the cards were turned he lost/ He asked if there was anyone who would bet a thousand on the next turn of the cards/ I then thought it was got up to deceive some greenhorn and that it was some accomplice who was winning from him. All the others present thought so too/ None of them would venture to bet and he had to go on as usual betting twenty on the turn of the cards/ His bad luck still followed him/ He lost every time and at last his money being all gone he pulled off his coat and put it up against ten dollars/ Again the cards were thrown and again the gambler lost/ He now pulled out a splendid looking gold watch and chain and put it up against one hundred. It was frightful to watch the fearful workings of his countenance as he again turned up the cards/ Again he lost and with a fearful imprecation he dashed down the cards and rushed from the hall a ruined gambler.

Many scenes of the opposite kind were taking place in another place in another part of the hall/ Here you would see a man in a rough miner's suit putting his bag of dust on the single turn of a color/ In a moment it would be decided and the greedy gambler would rake in the proceeds of many weeks' or months' hard labor. With a fierce oath the unhappy man would turn away and go and dig for more dust to be squandered in the same manner/

For about an hour I stopped in that den of temptation and crime and in that time I saw many painful scenes/ I have seen the hard earnings of toil swept in a few moments into the gambler's possession. For the case I mentioned is the exception and not the rule/ Gamblers scarcely ever lose when they play with outsiders/ In that case I think he was cleaned by gamblers in disguise.

They try all stratagems to decoy the unwary/ One of the most common dodges is for one of themselves to dress up in rough miner's clothes straggle up to the table look on awhile make clownish remarks about the game and after a while they place a five dollar on some card/ The card wins of course/ He doubles it. It wins again/ He increases his bets always winning and at last he says he will not risk any more and agrees to give his place to anybody else/ Some greenhorn lays down a twenty on the winning card and in a moment the cards are turned up again and he has lost. In hopes to retrieve his fortune he plays again/ Again he is beaten and so on every time until the unfortunate wretch is ruined. The temptation is almost irresistible/

A gambler takes three cards shows you the face of them turns them over on the table changes them a few times and then if you think you know where any particular card is you can lay down your pile [and] call out the name of the card/ If it is the one you call the banker hands you over the amount of your bet/ If not he rakes in the whole. I went farther down the hall and saw women engaged behind the tables gaudily dressed trying to decoy the poor greenhorn into their toils. All kinds of games were going on/ The crowds were in good spirits and bets were running high/ Thousands of dollars were changing hands at every turn of the cards.

I soon grew weary of the exciting scene and made for the open air for relief from the wretched sight of that abode of crime. We walked around the streets for I did not wish to risk going in to see another of those dens of infamy/ We passed several of them and saw crowds pouring in at the doors/ It seemed as if in this place men were careless of money/ They got it so easy. It seemed to burn in their pockets till it was all gone and then they cheerfully go to work for more.

The next day our friend William Clancy arrived in town/ He was just from the gold regions of Gregory and gave us a very gloomy picture indeed of gold mining and our prospects/ He advised us to sell our goods (we could then get an enormous price for them) realize all the money we could and start back to the States. We would not consider such a proposition for a moment/ He then said if we were bound to go to the mountains that the best place for us was to go to the Arkansas diggings, about one hundred and eighty miles from Denver. He said it was a new discovery reported very rich and the immigration towards that place was not very numerous as yet/ So that day we made up our minds to start on the next morning for the Arkansas.

Chapter III

The End of the Rainbow:
Blue River Diggings

WE made all necessary preparations and started at daylight for the mountains about fifteen miles distant. The gigantic mass of earth seemed to be raising out of the earth every step we took towards it, By noon we had made only eight miles and when we camped it seemed as far off as it was in the morning, Its tremendous peaks covered with eternal snow hung threateningly over our heads and were in sight hundreds of miles north and south. We stopped only a short time for dinner and took another start, The country here was slightly undulating but not enough to be called hilly and preserved the same aspect to the very base of the mountains. I think that is very remarkable for in the neighborhood of most mountains the country for fifty miles from their base is very rough and hilly but here it was nice meadow land to the very mountains itself.

It was about sundown when we camped at the very foot of the mountains, We chose a nice green spot where a small stream or mountain torrent which took its rise in those grim icy regions above us ran laughing by us. It was a most magnificent sight. The setting sun tinged those gloomy heights with his golden yellow the white snow seemingly about to fall upon our heads, the slopes of the mountains rising tier above tier covered with green pine and fir trees and on the other hand lay stretched the boundless prairie that we had traversed. Denver City was plainly in sight although fifteen miles distant. The Platte River could be seen like a silver thread winding its course along the bosom of the prairie. We pitched our camp staked out our horses got ready some supper and then had leisure to view the stupendous wonders around us.

It was a glorious moonlight night, The air soft and warm as summer and the mountains looked grand and weird looking. The scene would almost inspire one with superstition and dread. We built a large fire [and] sat around it, We did not need it as the air was warm enough but we always considered it more sociable, The prairie traveler considers it lonely not to have a fire even the hottest days in summer. We sat and talked till late that night, Each one related all that he had heard or read about that huge frowning pile before us. Some told of dangers hardships and privations of parties starting to cross them and they were never heard of afterwards, stories of wild animals and hostile Indians, till we got our imaginations worked up to that pitch that we could almost imagine that those gloomy piles were peopled by evil and malignant spirits. Still if it was so it would not deter people from going there in search of the shining ore which scarcely ever

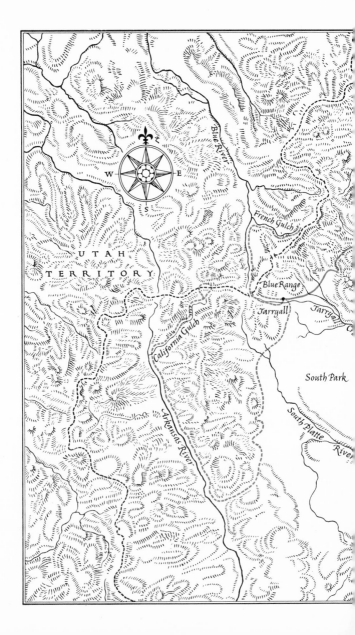

WHERE
YOUNG
PROSPECTED

CODE

ROUTE TRAVELED
CONJECTURED ROUTE
CONTINENTAL DIVIDE AND
TERRITORIAL BOUNDARY

brings happiness to its possessor. At a late hour in
the night we lay down by our campfires to sleep but
it did not visit my eyelids for some hours after, I
could not close my eyes on the beautiful appearance
of those mountains.

I had a refreshing night's sleep and awoke in the
morning about daybreak, The rest of the boys were
already up and busy preparing to make a start into
the mountains, but we remarked it as somewhat
singular that although it was an hour after daylight
and a clear sky there was no appearance of the sun's
rising, On examining our compass we found that
a high spur of mountains stood between us and the
east and it was two hours after daylight before old Sol
peeped over its summit. By this time we had all things
prepared and commenced to climb the old Rockies.

We entered through a defile or mountain gully,
The dried up bed of a stream there was still a small
rivulet running in its lowest parts, On either hand
rose towering precipices that would make the eye
ache to look to their summits. The ascent was very
gradual for the first two miles but a steady incline
upward. At this point the mountains presented a
most sublime view huge rocks piled tier above tier
thousands of feet above our heads threatening at
the slightest jar or puff of wind to rush resistlessly
down to our destruction. Along by our feet rushed
a small mountain torrent, Its water cold and clear
as crystal refreshed our lips many times during that
weary ascent.

We continued on till about noon and made probably six miles on our journey. As soon as we entered the mountains we lost altogether our view of the plains, Our compass was the only means of knowing in what direction we were going, Our main course so far was southwest. At the spot where we camped for dinner there was scarcely room for our wagons to stand, The mountains rose on both sides of us almost perpendicular, The road made in the bottom was only just wide enough for one wagon. After a rest of a couple of hours we commenced to climb again, The road commenced to get very rough and stony and some places very steep hills to climb so very steep that we would have to get four teams of horses to pull us up.

It was very slow going now and shortly before sunset finding a level spot of ground we camped for the night. We made only three miles this afternoon making nine in all and the hardest day's journey we had yet performed. I was so fatigued and wearied out that I threw myself full length upon the grass and fell asleep before supper. If this was to be a sample of a mountain road we were led to believe it was a good mountain road if so Lord help us when we got where there was no road. It was enough to make a man despair to think of having to travel one hundred and eighty miles of road worse than that, for we were informed that the first part of the road was the best.

We got our supper and then gathered some dry pine logs which were here in abundance to keep up a good fire for the night, Although only an hour after dark and nine miles into the mountains the indications were that we would have some frost before morning. So we started a huge fire brought out our buffalo skins and blankets and fixed our sleeping places for the night. We were obliged to sleep in the open air for we could not find level space enough to spread our tent and picketed our horses set the watch and things being all right lay down and took our first snooze on the Rocky Mountains,

No one who has not experienced it can imagine the delicious feeling that comes over the weary traveler who has toiled up steep mountain sides all day when he throws himself down to repose at night on his hard bed with nothing but the sky for a covering. I have lain on my back for hours watching those numberless stars ever changing their positions, the moon sailing brightly through milk white clouds, the beautiful "Milky Way" showing like a belt of silver across the sky. In this place it shows clearer and brighter than in any other part of the world, tall spires and peaks raising their snow capped peaks heavenward in all directions and on every side. It is here in such a place as this that the heart turns to admiration at the skill of the wonderful Creator of all these wonders.

After journeying about four days more the country became so mountainous that we were forced to make two parts of our loads. We built a small hut in the woods by the roadside put in about half our provisions and leaving two of our party in charge we started once more on our journey.[23] We were now on the most elevated range of the mountains/ All around us was clouds and snow/ The air was very oppressive/ After climbing a small hill you would pant like a sheep on a hot day/ The height of this dividing range is about eighteen thousand feet. In the afternoon after leaving our companions we commenced to descend very rapidly/ We continued going down all the afternoon/

In the evening we reached the Platte River which we found to be the last of our descending. The river here is thirty miles in a straight line from the outside of the mountains and about a mile higher/ It is a huge mountain torrent at this time roaring and tumbling tearing trees and rocks along in its headlong course/ Yet we camped on its banks having the cheerless prospect of having to ford it early in the morning.

I never camped yet during the whole trip with more complete lowness of spirits/ We had left part of our company behind/ Probably we would never see them again. We met parties returning from the mountains who gave unfavorable accounts of the mines. They also reported that the Indians were showing signs of hostility and gave it as their opinion that they would massacre all the white men on

[23]Kerwin and Mullen (McMullen). "Leave part of loads in the woods with me & and [sic] Joseph McMullen[.] the rest goe on to Tarihaul[.]" Entry for June 1, 1860, Kerwin diary.

the mountains/ Add to all these the knowledge that dangers and difficulties were increasing every day on the road we began to think that we would have to abandon our wagons and pack our provisions through. On a cold mountain side cold and shivering no covering from the night air it was as cheerless a prospect as any one can imagine. At that time if I was at home with the same experience acquired I think nothing could induce me to leave the comforts of home for the dangers and difficulties of gold hunting.

In the morning we got up very early to prepare for crossing the river/ We had breakfast before daylight/ Sometimes the sun would raise over the hills before ten o'clock. We put four teams to one wagon and started towards the ford/ The river was about ten yards wide and about as deep as the wagon bed the bottom being made of great stones carried down by the force of the water. It was a miniature Niagara/ The roaring of the water made our voices inaudible as we rushed our horses madly into the stream/ The only chance to get over without capsizing is to cross it quick as the horses can gallop. We got the first wagon across in glorious style and [up] the steep hill on the other side before the horses could be stopped/ We had to then go back again with the teams for the other three wagons/ They were all brought over in the same manner.

We were now in a terrible rough place/ The road lay over huge rocks/ Sometimes the wagon would have to jump from rock to rock, I thought every moment it would smash to pieces, After making about two miles we again came to the Platte River, Our course lay straight across it and we had the same labor in again crossing it. The reason we had to cross the same river twice was because the only practicable road lay in the valleys and we had to travel there no matter how much longer the road was nor what obstacles lay in the way. We crossed the same river no less than five times on that day and twice on the next day making nine times in all.[24] The sufferings and hardships we endured on each occasion of crossing cannot be described on paper. Sometimes the wagon would get fast in the middle of the stream probably wedged against a great stone that came down with the flood, Then we would have to wade into the stream and with crowbar and levers pry it out of the way. The water was icy cold and when we came out the chill mountain air would stiffen us up with cold,

To make matters worse a snow storm set in with great severity, The clouds rested on the very mountain tops so very dense that they obscured the view before us making it very dangerous to follow a

[24] Young is apparently progressing westward in the valley of the North Fork of the South Platte River. This route is shown on "Map of Colorado Showing Location of Mining Districts . . .," Charles W. Henderson, *Mining in Colorado: A History of Discovery, Development and Production* (U.S. Geological Survey, *Professional Paper 138*, Washington, 1926), Plate I, pocket.

mountain road any longer. We turned in by the roadside and secured a sheltry place for our cattle/ Pitched our tent sheltered by a friendly stunted pine tree and got our stove into it and soon had a rousing fire/ One thing was in our favor there being plenty of dry pine wood laying in the shelter of the rocks.

We were now comparatively comfortable/ I felt as good sheltered from the storm by our canvas tent as if I lay in the most luxurious palace of my native city. We cooked some fresh venison that we got that day, made some warm biscuit and a good cup of tea and had a most comfortable supper with the storm howling madly around us on the highest range of the Rocky Mountains. After supper we built a huge fire sat closely around it and enjoyed ourselves by talking and singing for a couple of hours/ The time passed as joyous and light hearted as if we were at a splendid hall in the city. After a time we rolled ourselves up in our blankets and had a most comfortable night's sleep.

In the morning we found the roof of our tent almost borne down by the pressure of snow that had fallen during the night. As soon as I got out of the tent I found the ground covered with snow to the depth of about ten inches. It was a tough looking job to go out in that deep drift to look for some dry wood but we had to do it or freeze/ After hunting round for about an hour we found a log lying under a huge rock/ We carried it to the tent and in a short time had a rousing fire.

After breakfast we started again on our journey, This day and the next two passed without any incident, The mountains traveled were having the same rough appearance as those passed over previously, Sometimes we had very severe labor in getting up hills and one time going down the hill was so steep that the brakes were not sufficient to stop the wagon and we had to rope to the trees to keep them from being dashed to pieces. We had now entered sixty miles into the mountains and we were getting heartily tired of the monotony of hills and valleys, All the time I thought the prairies tiresome and dreary but they are fine compared to the mountains, The constant grandeur of them ever before around and above you brings on a surfeit and you long to see a few acres of level ground.

On the third afternoon after leaving the Platte we were journeying slowly along up and down the rocks, We climbed up one rougher than usual wound slowly round its lofty base when suddenly on rounding its corner I thought for a moment that I was flying through the air, A most grand and magnificent sight burst on our view looking like a vast sea dotted here and there the Great Central Park of the Rocky Mountains lying stretched at our feet.[25] I thought it was the grandest sight I had ever beheld, It seemed as if we had been journeying ofttime through dangers difficulties and storms and at last had reached the haven of peace. We all stood en-

[25]This mountain-rimmed meadow called South Park is largely in Park County, Colorado. *Ibid.*, 24.

tranced bewildered for a few moments gazing intently down upon the splendid scene/ Then we had to give vent to our feelings in some way so we shouted with all our might peal upon peal for several minutes.

At last getting calmed down a little we made a few observations before descending into the park. It looked to be a vast plain level as a lake having beautiful streams dotting its surface in all directions/ It was seemingly eighty miles long thirty broad bound on all sides by the blue snow capped mountains on one of which we were standing. We stood admiring the scenery for about half an hour and then prepared to descend/ Our walk lay directly across it/ It was plainly in sight for twenty miles. This is a most remarkable freak of nature in the center of the Rocky Mountains at an elevation of eight thousand feet above the sea to find a broad level prairie grass growing there luxuriantly and not a hill on all its broad surface to mar its level surface/ It has a wonderful effect upon the mountain voyageur after having enough mountains for many days.

We now commenced to descend for we stood on a mountain spur about one thousand feet higher than the plane/ The descent was very abrupt and we had to tie three of our wheels to keep the wagon from pitching over upon the horses/ In about two hours we reached the park and found that it was even lovelier looking than we had imagined while looking upon it from the mountain top. The grass was soft and green as a meadow in our own prairie state, Nice little brooks clear as crystal filled with brook trout sporting gaily before our eyes crossed and recrossed each other all over the surface of the plain,

Everything looking so invitingly comfortable we made up our minds to camp there for the night. We picketed out our horses and for the first time in four weeks they had good grass, We made a spear and caught some fine brook trout for supper, That evening we had such a supper as might make an epicure envious of our enjoyment, fish, flesh, and fowls, the kinds being the trout, venison and buffalo meat with some bacon to supply the grease for cooking and then we had some ducks, For the dessert we made some warm biscuits and tea and it was really the most comfortable meal we had on the journey.

This night we did not suffer any from cold, We were sheltered from the winds by the mountains, In the morning we started once more on a smooth level road, It continued very good until noon when we came to a swamp or morass similar to those in Illinois, It was about a fourth of a mile across and dreadful hard pulling, Sometimes I thought we must sink and go under the mud, We held on bravely and at last got across safe, We then journeyed on and arrived at Tarryall[26] an hour before sunset, This is

[26] Tarryall was located on Tarryall Creek some four miles northwest of present Como. Later the present town of Tarryall was established in eastern Park County. Norma L. Flynn, "Early Mining Camps of South Park," in Nolie Mumey, ed., *Original Contributions to Western History* (*The Westerners Brand Book, 1951*, Denver, 1952), 123–126.

one hundred miles from Denver and eighty miles from the place we entered them. It took us just ten days to come that distance. We were now at the mining ground the goal of all our hopes and expectations and when we came to look at the prospects it seemed as if we were as far as ever from realizing the acquiring of gold which had brought us so long a journey.

Tarryall [is] so-called from its being the terminus of the wagon road and the starting point from which you could go to the Blue or Arkansas river diggings. Tarryall had some pretensions to be called a town/ They had the plat all staked out into lots. There was about forty houses erected and ten more in course of construction/ The ranches seemed to have a full stock of groceries and provisions and doing a pretty smart business.

It was a pretty lively town/ There was a large tent big enough for to contain Dan River's "Big Show" with all kinds of gambling apparatus there and a large crowd always present pursuing the delusive phantom. Another place you could see a Mexican leading fifteen or twenty jacks and bawling out at the top of his voice for some freight to carry over to the different gulches. Miners were to be met here in crowds rough looking as if they had lived in those mountains for twenty years. Some were coming to town to spend their pile of dust and others were you could tell it from their looks disappointed and were going in search of new diggings. The latter were by far the greater number and their personal appearance was in most cases wretched in the extreme.

I think gold seeking is the most uncertain and precarious business in the world as man is tempted and risks so much that he would not do in following other pursuits. If he has a claim in a remote place far away from any place where he could purchase provisions he will be tempted to stay working on that claim from day to day until his last mouthful of provisions is exhausted, Then without anything to eat he will undertake a journey of twenty or thirty miles over mountains covered with snow and sometimes by paths unknown to him depending upon luck only to keep him from starvation. Your real gold hunter is the most careless fellow in existence, He thinks of gold sleeping and waking and new reported discoveries will excite his imagination and carry him off even at midnight to secure a claim without making any provision for the difficulties and dangers of the way,

It was now growing dark so I had to leave farther observation for tomorrow and go back to camp. Our camp was on the banks of the Tarryall River the waters of which was very yellow caused by the miners washing their dirt in the stream about two miles above. This night passed away pleasantly like the one before it not cold in the least.

In the morning I took an early start up Tarryall Gulch to see the mining operations. We passed through the town climbed some very rugged hills

Sluice Box, Tarryall Placers, date unknown

and then found ourselves at the mines/ The first time any of our party had ever seen gold washed. The process is very simple/ All that is necessary is to turn the bed of the river which is done by making a tail ditch and running the water into a new channel/ Then you remove the boulder stones from the bed of the stream sometimes a work of great labor some of them being so large that you must break them with a sledge hammer and remove them in pieces/ After getting them clear you then have to strip the earth off down to the bedrock/ Sometimes it is only two feet and sometimes it may be twelve or fourteen.

The dirt laying close to the rock is what is called the pay dirt/ You will have to shovel that into your sluice a long box about from fifty to five hundred feet long with a small stream of water running through it and riffles placed near the end charged with quicksilver to catch the gold. The earth is shoveled in from the gulch runs down the whole length of the sluice carried along by the force of the water when it gets to the riffles/ The lighter particles will roll over the riffles but the gold being the heaviest will drop down and amalgamate with the quicksilver which is placed at the bottom of the riffles to receive it. You may keep shoveling all day/ Then you take out your riffles squeeze your quicksilver in a rag and the gold will separate from it/ You then take your quicksilver and put it into a bottle/ It only loses twenty per cent by using. What remains then is gold having only a small alloy of black sand.

The scene now before us was a busy one every claim being taken up/ The size of the claim is one hundred feet up and down the gulch running into the hills clear to the extremity of the mountains if you wished to go so far. I made some inquiries about the value of claims. They asked from five hundred to ten thousand dollars. It was apparently very hard work/ The stripping was about ten feet deep hard boulder stone loosened with a pickax/ The water came in on them in spite of their best endeavors and they had to work in cold ice water often up to the knees. The gulch was about two miles long extending almost to the summit of the Blue Range of mountains.[27] Near the upper end they had no water and had to carry the dirt about one fourth of a mile to wash it/ Evidently it was richer than that at the lower part/ Out of two tons of dirt as much as two men could carry in a day they generally washed about twenty dollars. I took particular notice of the preparation for opening a claim and the washing and saving of gold and all other matters that I thought might be of interest in the new career opening before me/ At evening we returned to the camp or as we called it home. Had a good supper and then rolled up in our blankets to sleep away the day's fatigues.

[27] This is probably Hoosier Ridge stretching from Hoosier Pass on the southwest to Boreas Pass on the northeast along the Continental Divide on the Summit–Park county boundary line.

In the morning we were up early and got our teams ready and dispatched them along with two drivers for our comrades and provisions which we had left behind. Until their return which I knew must be four or five days I determined to start out and if possible find some place where we could secure a claim/ Another of the party agreeing to go with me we made all ready/ Packed our provisions for two weeks on the back of a mule/ Strapped our blankets on our backs and started at about noon for the Blue River diggings about sixteen miles distant and across a high snowy range of mountains which were then plainly in sight and most dreary and forbidding looking/

We passed by Tarryall and continued up the gulch in a western direction. We had a comparatively smooth road for about three miles. Then we commenced to ascend the middle or dividing range between Kansas and Utah.[28] And indeed it was a most formidable looking barrier from where we now stood/ Grand gloomy and frowning the sight was enough to deter a stout heart from attempting to scale those forbidding and seemingly impassible barriers of ice and snow. We kept boldly on our course and by night we camped just at the snow line.

We set ourselves to work busily gathering wood for the night for we anticipated a severe night's frost/ After a good deal of labor we got enough

[28] The Continental Divide was the boundary between the two territories.

kindled a fire made some coffee and had a lunch/
We picketed out our mule and then rolling our
blankets around us and laying down by the fire we
were comfortably prepared for a night's sleep. You
may think it curious that I say comfortable but such
was really the fact/ After the fatigue of walking
about six miles up hill with your knees aching every
step you took it was a luxury to get lying down any-
where especially as the night was cold and chilly/
I thought it a most comfortable position rolled up
in my blanket by a good fire and with no shelter
over us but the broad heavens. We lay there and
chatted for a long time/ It was getting very cold and
we rolled so close to the fire as to singe our blankets/

Shortly after this my companion fell asleep/ I
could not on account of the cold/ Do what I could
and I could not have more than one half of me
warm at a time the side that was towards the fire the
other side would be freezing. I felt very lonesome/
A feeling of desolation came over me as I thought
of the isolation of our position, two persons who had
never been out of a large city before now sleeping
on the summit of and amid the eternal snows of the
Rocky Mountains. Near morning I got a short doze/

I woke up at daylight shivering and benumbed
from the cold/ I felt an unusual weight on my body
and on pushing the blanket from my head I perceived
that we had a heavy fall of snow during the night.
Things looked wretched in the extreme/ Our fire
was entirely extinguished/ The wretched mule stood

near by covered with a white blanket of snow so weak and exhausted by hunger and cold that he was not able to shake the snow from his back. I aroused my comrade and we set out on a cruise to look for some dry wood/ Fortunately we found some close by and in a few minutes we had a rousing fire/ I enjoyed it hugely/ I was nearly perished/ Even the poor mule came alongside and warmed one side and then turned round the other/ He seemed to enjoy it as much as we did.

We prepared some breakfast and by sunrise were once more ascending towards that far off lofty peak/ The trail was entirely obliterated by the snow that had fallen during the night/ We now had to guide our course by a pocket compass/ It now became awful hard to go ahead/ Sometimes we would get into drifts over our armpits/ There was also great danger of walking over some concealed precipice and being dashed to pieces/ The mule showed signs of giving out and I thought we must have the poor thing to perish on the mountains. We sat down nearly in despair at the cheerless looking prospect when we heard some merry voices ahead and seemingly coming towards us/ In a few minutes they reached us and I found among them some friends who had traveled with us on the road/

They told us it was impossible to bring our mule any farther and they offered to take him back to our camp/ We accepted their offer thankfully/ They then gave us some advice about and how to avoid the heavy drifts/ They had camped about a mile down on the western side of the mountains and said they had no snow that night/ They were in good spirits about their prospects over on the Blue/ They had taken claims and were going to Tarryall for tools and provisions/ They started down the mountain and in a few minutes were out of sight in a deep valley.

We now had to arrange our packs and make them as convenient as possible to carry on our shoulders/ We had each a pair of blankets weighing about five pounds each ten pounds of flour three pounds of meat two pounds of sugar one pound of coffee a coffee pot and frying pan making in all about fifteen pounds for each to carry. We strapped the bundles on our shoulders and started bravely up the mountain. The sun now shone out pretty hot melting the snow and making it very disagreeable/ The summit now was about a mile off but it did not look one fourth that distance/ The incline was becoming more steep so that we had to sit down and rest about every fifteen yards.

Oh it was terrible hard work climbing up there/ Sometimes I would fix a point and say we would make that our next resting place/ We would start and strain every sinew to reach it but it would be impossible/ Ere we got half way we would be panting like a sheep on a hot day/ Our knees would get weak and shaky and we would drop down utterly exhausted and lay full length on the snow until we would get revived. The pack small as it was by this time had grown into an enormous burden/ We thought if we were rid of it that we could make the journey without much inconvenience and we were almost tempted to throw it away. The fact of it is a man is not so strong up on these great heights/ The air is pure and rare and what would be only on level ground only a recreation at these great heights throws a man into the same way as would running or any other violent exercises.

About noon we reached the summit/ We rested there and had some dinner/ The scenery from the point was beautiful and sublime/ We could see peak upon peak many hundreds of them all snow covered stretching away in every direction/ They were such a bright shining color from the sun shining upon them as almost to dazzle the eye. Although upon the summit or dividing ridge of the mountains we were not upon the highest point/ Many peaks around us were thousands of feet higher, but from the spot where we were resting the water from under our feet caused by melted snow runs some of it into the Pacific Ocean and some of it into the Gulf of Mexico/ We followed it down the western slope until it forms the Blue River from thence to Grand River then into the Colorado and the Gulf of California/ On the eastern side I have traced it to the Platte River from thence to the Mississippi and to the Gulf of Mexico.

We stayed there about half an hour/ It began to look very like snow so we hastily packed up and started down the mountain, Our wanderings had at last brought us into the Territory of Utah. We now continued our journey without much farther inconvenience and in about three hours arrived at the Blue River diggings,[29] It was nearly night and we could not look up any friends so we built a fire close to where there was a company of miners and prepared to pass another night in the open air. There was no snow here but the air was raw and cold and froze some before morning. There seemed to be a great crowd of miners here judging by the noise they raised after supper, Such hooting yelling and screaming I have not heard in a long time, All seemed to be enjoying themselves, I passed round through several camps, They were singing songs cracking jokes and passing round the whisky pretty freely, They appeared to be very friendly and always said "Stranger take a drink." I did not find any one that I knew but I made some inquiries about the prospects of the place, The miners all seemed to be contented, If they were making nothing they lived in hopes of doing it before many days, They claimed that the diggings were as good as any other in the mountains.

This night we had a shelter to get under, Some miners seeing us about camping out for the night very kindly asked us to sleep in their shanty an of-

---

[29]The Blue River diggings and French Gulch, which Young was to visit shortly, were in Summit County, Colorado. Henderson, *Mining in Colorado*, 32–33.

*Blue River Diggings, 1860s, some time after
Young's prospecting visit*

Placer Mining in Colorado, 1860s, location unknown

fer which we very gladly accepted as the night was very cold/ We had comparatively a comfortable sleep and arose in the morning fresh as if we had not climbed the highest range of the Rocky Mountains on the previous day.

Mining was going on extensively in this place/ On the Blue River alone there was about one thousand claims taken/ None of them any good remained unoccupied. The way the mining was carried on was by sluicing. There was first a tail ditch dug into which the river was turned/ Then they removed the boulder and stripped the earth in the bed of the stream down to the bedrock. Then they made a sluice a box having three sides made of pine boards bought in this place at a cost of two hundred dollars per thousand feet. The top of the sluice was then inserted into the stream and about one inch deep of water allowed to run through it. All being now ready they shovel the pay dirt into the sluice/ All worthless matter is carried off/ The gold remains at the bottom of the sluice/ I described minutely in a previous page of this the process of collecting and saving gold.

There was a log fort built on this gulch for the protection of the whites in case the Indians should commence hostilities/ They were assuming a very threatening attitude being collected about five miles from here fifteen hundred in number. The fort was a very strong looking building being made of large pine logs about ten feet high inclosing about one acre and loopholed on every side for musketry.

As there was not any chance of getting a claim here I determined to start for a new discovery about five miles off called French Gulch, It was said to be very rich and not many claims taken there as yet. The sun was about two hours high when we started, The road was pretty good and we got to the gulch just at dark. As good fortune would have it the first man I made inquiries of proved to be the very friend I had been in search of, He welcomed me most heartily invited us into his wigwam and treated us with the greatest of friendship. He said he did not think much of his gulch, There was gold all through it but not in large enough quantities to pay for opening a claim, Although he had claims to dispose of he would not encourage us to take from him or to stop on the gulch at all. He said he would try and sell his claims and then go over to the Arkansas.

We had a jolly night of it some eight or ten merry fellows all as merry light hearted and free from care as if they were pursuing a fireside occupation at home instead of encountering all the dangers sufferings and hardships of a miner's life. They had not provisions for more than two days and if a heavy snowstorm set in in the meantime it might be some weeks before they could get over to the Blue for a supply, I thought it recklessness of the grossest kind, they did not feel very uneasy but said that if it did snow they would get out of it in some way. A few days before that they were up in a narrow gulch prospecting, A fire swept down upon them like an avalanche not giving them time to save any of their provisions and barely time to escape with their lives. After enjoying ourselves for a couple of hours we rolled up in our blankets and had a night's refreshing sleep.

In the morning we started on a prospecting tour carrying a shovel pick and gold pan, We started up the gulch towards the snowy range taking provisions for two days. We traveled about two hours and then coming to what we considered a promising looking place we cleared off a space and dug a small hole down as far as the bedrock which was here about five feet deep. We then took up the "pay dirt" the earth next the bedrock and washed a pan full or about a peck of clay. The process of washing is to carry it to a stream of running water sink your pan holding it in your hands all the time and gently tilting it from side to side. The current carries off all the sand and clay and light particles leaving the heavier ones or the black sand a composition of iron and the gold if there is any, By using a magnet you can then separate the sand from the gold.

You may think that the gold can escape as well as the other particles but it is not so, Take an experienced gold washer and put grain of dust weighing only one cent into a bushel of earth, Mix it up thoroughly and he can wash that heap of dirt and find that small piece of gold. It may seem incredible but you must understand that gold is so heavy that water cannot carry it along. I have seen a nugget weighing two penny weights put into a mountain torrent running ten miles an hour and although it was placed upon a flat board the water could not carry it along or overturn it.

In our prospect this time we found a pretty good color but not rich enough to warrant us in staking out claims. To be rich enough to pay us five dollars a day you must wash from a claim with a gold pan about three cents to the pan/ Earth that will yield that much I think would be safe enough to work by sluicing.

We gave up that place picked up our traps and proceeded on our tour/ We prospected several times that day but found nothing better than the first one. In every hole we found the color/ The gold is scattered through those mountains so that you cannot dig any where without finding the color but it is extremely rare to find a place rich enough to repay a man for his labor in getting it out.

We camped out that night about ten miles from where we started/ We built a shanty of pine limbs/ Built a good fire in front and just at dark we were as snug and comfortable a party of gold hunters as could be found on the mountains. One of our party had killed two jackass rabbits during the day/ We dressed and stewed them with some bacon/ Had some slap jacks as we called them and made a first rate supper/ At that time I thought if I had all the wealth and luxuries the world could bestow that I never would wish for a better meal/ It was all that any poor hungry miner could wish for. We sat a long time at our meal/ The laugh and song went round/ We were as merry and light hearted a party of miners as could be found that night on the mountains. About midnight we rolled in our blankets the bright fire shining all around us/

We slept soundly the remainder of the night and roused early in the morning/ Had some breakfast and commenced again prospecting/ We had no better success than on the previous day so we concluded to give it up and take the back trail to camp again. We reached the camp just at dusk, hungry and tired out/ The boys had a good supper just prepared/ We sat down and done full justice to it/ After that we had a long talk with our host about the prospects of the diggings/ He candidly advised us to not stay a day longer on the place. I was fully satisfied myself that it would not pay to open a claim there so we determined to strike the back trail on the following morning.

We took an early start with the intention of crossing the range and gaining our camp before night/ It was about twenty miles distant. It was a most beautiful day the sky clear blue and cloudless. The trail had been so much traveled that the top was hard enough to bear us up and the traveling was comparatively easy. At about ten A.M. we came to the summit of the range/ After that it was a descent for about ten miles/ We encountered no difficulties worth speaking of and arrived at our camp at Tarryall about an hour before sunset.

The remainder of our party had got back safe bringing all the provisions with them/ We were now relieved of that cause of anxiety and could devote all our energies to the finding of a profitable claim. I stayed at camp a day to recruit after the fatigues of the journey/ We held a council of war concerning the future movements of our journey/ We concluded that on the next morning we would start off prospecting in all directions two together and leave one to mind the camp and horses. It was safe enough to leave them in charge of one because there was plenty of friends in our neighborhood who would lend him assistance if needed. This afternoon was a very busy time preparing our packs for the journey/ We were not going to take mules with us any more/ We found from experience that they were very inconvenient/ The best way is to take only what you absolutely need and carry that on your shoulder.

The equipment of a prospecting party is rather novel and when in full dress resembles a porcupine/ First comes the arms in a belt round the waist consisting of a revolver and a dirk knife/ The clothing is big boots a pair of buckskin pants a gray flannel shirt and a broad brimmed hat [which] completed our picturesque costume. Then our pack consisted of a pair of blankets and provisions suspended over our shoulders held by a stick a tin cup frying pan and coffee pot that completed our house keeping furniture. We had also to carry a compass shovel and pick and a gold pan/ Enough you may think to load a jack or mule. To meet a fellow in full regimentals as we used to style it you might imagine yourself in the primitive ages when they traveled from place to place carrying their household goods on their backs.

We had a good time of it that evening, All our party were at home, There was a good many dangers to be incurred on the journey we were on the eve of making and it might be that we should never all meet again, We talked over the intended routes that we were going to take and all of [us] agreed if possible to meet in the same place in two weeks time. I was detailed to the Arkansas diggings on the head of the Arkansas River, We broke up early and each one rolled up in his blanket prepared for an early start in the morning.

Chapter IV

The End of the Rainbow:
California Gulch

WE were all up early and preparing for the road, My comrade and myself did not take much provision along as we were informed that the diggings were only twenty five miles across the range by the pack trail and eighty by the wagon road, We were told that the trail was very faint in some places and that we should have to look sharp or we would get lost. All being ready we to make a start some of our friends came along and laughed at us for packing on our shoulders, They said that the trail was first rate and advised us to take a mule along, Their councils prevailed although I was certain that we should be sorry and we fixed up a mule and brought him along. So we packed all our traps on jack and started on our journey.

Our course lay westward across the broad level park to where a lofty peak lifted its snow capped summit to the sky, We were told to keep to the left-hand side of that peak and by looking very close we could find the trail. We journeyed along for some hours, What seemed only a short way lengthened out into miles but we camped at noon at the base of the peak, We had some dinner refreshed our mule and left the wagon road and struck for the left side of the peak as directed, We traveled on some hours finding faint trails, Very often we could not tell whether they were made by deer or Christians, We followed several of them winding round and round hills and then suddenly we would lose all trace of them. We were bewildered that way for a long time,

Finally we concluded that we would no longer follow their devious windings but pursue a straight course west by the compass, I knew that the Arkansas lay west and I would leave it to fate to bring us out in the right place. We now struck out boldly facing the steep hills and going as fast as we could, It was an awful wild looking place, The pine trees were growing too thick and so many of them were laying down blown by the hurricanes which frequently sweep over the mountains. We had the greatest difficulty in getting forward, To make matters worse we were now getting into the snow regions and in climbing a hill we would sometimes slip back again. We kept on bravely till night,

Just at twilight I spied on the other side of a torrent a pine shanty such as miners put up for a night's shelter, I thought it was a lucky thing for us, so we started over to take possession, But when I got there I was greatly shocked by finding that the shanty already had a tenant one who should occupy it until the last trump shall sound. Right in the center was a newly dug grave, A small paper stuck unto a stake driven into the ground informed us that a party of prospectors passing that way a few days before had found a man lying dead there/ He was shot through the leg apparently by accident and undoubtedly had died from starvation his leg being broken and not having any food. The paper stated that his gun lay near him/ Also some cooking utensils pickax shovel and gold pan. There was a few dollars in money in his pockets with some papers telling his name all of which his friends could have by applying to a certain house in Denver City. It was a most horrible fate the poor fellow met living there probably some days suffering all the pangs of hunger cold and pain/ He must have died a hundred deaths in anticipation before he was released from suffering. It was a more cruel death than the greatest tyrant of old ever prepared for his enemies.

That spot was no resting place for us that night/ I could not stop there if I was forced to sleep in the snow all night/ We recrossed the torrent but it was growing so very dark we dared not travel any farther/ There was some tremendous precipices all around us so we camped about one hundred yards from the grave/ Camped on the cold bare ground. We gathered some pine logs made a rousing fire cooked some supper but it was done in silence/ We could not help thinking of the lonely sleeper near us and of his horrid and lingering fate.

During the evening I frequently thought of the dangerous situation we were in/ If a snowstorm came on during the night it would make our condition desperate, There would be no possibility of getting across the yawning chasms and precipices that obstructed our way. Fortunately the night was clear and a full moon was beaming gloriously upon us covering the hills and rocks around us as with a sheet of silver. There was a most magnificent view from [the] giddy height on which we were camped, All around us were huge piles of rocks which required the greatest care in ascending or descending, In the distance could be seen on every side lofty peaks piercing the very sky covered with snow and then the contrast of the deep dark valleys where the moonlight did not penetrate, looking like gloomy dungeons. It was such a sight as I can never forget, The isolation of our position, the uncertainty of our getting on to the trail again without having to retrace our steps, for I did not yet consider that we were lost as I thought we could go back again at any time but we would not do so, as we thought by keeping on a west course we must come out on the trail before long.

After a couple of hours chatting we rolled up in our blankets and lay down before the fire to get some sleep, We had performed a big day's journey and felt tired, The night was now getting pretty cold and our mule poor fellow having nothing to eat and probably feeling lonesome as well as ourselves came along and stood by the fire, We had not a morsel of food or grass for him that night. I lay on my back listening to the musical snoring of

my companion who was asleep almost as soon as
he lay down. I was musing on sublimity and grandeur of the surrounding objects, I felt very melancholy and sad, Thoughts of my far away home and
friends were rising in my heart, and I could not
help thinking of the lonely sleeper in the valley
below me, Perhaps some fond mother sister wife
and children were looking anxiously for tidings
from the absent one, Little they know that he is
sleeping his last sleep on the very summit of the
Rocky Mountains.

I could not go to sleep, I lay for some hours
thinking in this way of one thing or another, At
last I was just dozing off and in a semiconscious
state my face was turned up partly covered by the
blanket when I felt a warm breath on my face, I
started opened my eyes instantly and saw a sight
that startled me so much that I yelled out, It was
the mule looking into my face with his nose just
touching mine, The poor fellow wanted com-
panionship but you cannot imagine how horrible
looking it was just as I opened my eyes to see by
the bright moonlight his great goggle eyes looking
into mine, I gave him a box in the head and sent
him off. After that you may be sure I could get no
sleep for some time again but towards morning I got
a small nap and got up at daylight much refreshed,

We had some breakfast and the last of our provisions before starting for you must remember we
took provisions for only one day expecting as it

was only twenty five miles to the Arkansas that we could get there in that time. It was an awful wild place we now had to travel through, The wind had swept through here at some time with dreadful violence prostrating trees in every direction. The trunks now lay on the ground some places held up three feet high by the limbs, We were obliged to climb over these obstacles and sometimes both legs of trousers and skin would suffer sorely. In other places we had tremendous snowdrifts to wade through, I have passed through some as high as my head. Our mule would get stuck in these and sink down so as to be almost covered, By letting him alone he would flounder out again, In other places there was huge rocks to climb, In places it would be perpendicular steps two or three feet high.

We toiled along over all these obstacles until as we calculated by the sun it was noon, We were now terribly hungry and the poor mule just as bad off, however there was no remedy for it but to push boldly forward. We were now greatly alarmed that perhaps we had lost our way entirely and might never get out of those inhospitable regions alive, It was madness to attempt to turn back for supposing we could find the way it took us a day and a half to come this far and in our present famished state we could not expect to reach camp in less than two days. Before that time I knew we would fall on the road and perish by starvation. We knew the certain doom that lay behind us so we had to push on at all hazards. We kept a sharp look out for game but could not get a shot at any thing/

We saw a few mountain goats and shot our rifles at them several times but without affect as they were out of range. The Rocky Mountain goat is a curious animal/ He delights in standing on some high inaccessible rock where nothing but the eagle can approach him/ There he will stay for hours bold haughty and defiant looking. When he wishes to descend he scorns to come down by jumping from rock to rock, but he takes a bold spring and into air and alights on his head/ The enormous bunch of bone or horns protects him from all injuries/ I have seen one of their horns at Tarryall that weighed eighty pounds. They are very shy and it is a rare thing to kill one of them. The flesh is good tasting like wild mutton.

About the middle of the afternoon we got terribly hungry/ If a prairie wolf could be captured we would not have stood on any ceremony about feasting on his carcass, but then if we were driven to extremity the mule would have to provide be sacrificed to preserve life, but we had neither of us spoken of such an alternative, but I know it was for that purpose we dragged the poor animal after us. He was so famished that if we would let him he would lay down never to raise again. I found that by tightening the belt which I wore around my body that it eased the pangs of hunger/ All prairie travelers will admit the fact by pulling up the strap another hole every time that hunger pinches you will husband your strength and not so soon have to surrender to the gnawing pangs of hunger.

Shortly after this time we had climbed an un-usual high hill and just as we got to the top we be-held a sight that drove terror into our hearts, Away down in the valley beneath us was a large encamp-ment of Indians. Before we left the camp we had rumors of hostilities between the Ute and the whites. Anyhow in the most peaceable time it would be dangerous to get into their camp away off in those wild regions where they were perfectly well aware they could commit any outrages they pleased on white men without any fears of retaliation. If we fell into their hands they would surely rob and perhaps murder us. Fortunately there was none of the Indians in sight, I suppose they kept no watch deeming themselves secure in such an inaccessible place,

We drew back instantly not knowing but that we were seen and pursued. We commenced descend-ing the hill with all the speed that we were capable of terror I suppose making us go quicker than we could under any other impulse for we imagined every moment that they were after us and several times I thought I heard the dreaded war whoop. It was not through cowardice that we ran in that manner, I believe if any danger threatened us where the odds were not too great against us that at the time we would not have turned down that hill again, but against that savage horde we would not have the least chance, If they pursued us we would have fired on the first of them and then we could expect no mercy. It was the most prudent thing we could do to get away quietly if possible.

We reached the bottom of the hill without any signs of pursuit and we began to hope they had not seen us, Still we must proceed with the greatest caution for where there was such a large number of Indians as was evident by their wigwams we were liable at any moment to meet some straggling parties on the hunt. We traveled cautiously keeping a sharp lookout, If we only heard a twig snap we stopped and reconnoitered in every direction before proceeding. We rounded the hill adding I suppose two miles to our journey and got unto our west course again without meeting any of the Indians.

The fright we got drove all thoughts of hunger out of our heads, I think if the excitement was kept up all day that we would not feel the least inconvenience from that source but when we considered ourselves safe having seen no signs of a pursuit hunger assailed us again more severely than at any previous time, Still we could not succeed in killing any kind of game.

We kept on our course till darkness set in, We were now in if possible a more gloomy place than last night, Tall forest trees hemmed us in at every side, Our view did not extend more than a few yards in every direction. We chose a sheltered spot and lay down for the night/ The mule commenced eating the tops of small pine trees/ He was even better off than us/ We could not get the least nourishment! If something did not turn up before another day we should have to preserve life by dining upon mule flesh. It was a pretty hard thing to take the poor faithful animal's life but necessity is above all law. I was so wearied out in body and mind that I soon fell asleep and forgot all my troubles/

I slept without awakening till after sunrise/ I found that my friend had done equally as well but on first getting on our feet we could hardly stand and for a few minutes we reeled about like drunken men from very weakness/ I felt sick at the stomach and dizziness in the head. Our mule was not in sight but we were sure he had not gone far because he was not able. We staggered around and found him in a short time, and once more turned our faces towards the West. The most depressing thoughts now run come into my head/ I thought that we were most certainly lost and that we were doomed to die in those gloomy mountains and our fate never be known.

About two hours after starting as we were walking slowly and sorrowfully along a plain of about a mile in extent we suddenly came across the trail without any indication of being in its neighborhood until we stood on it. Although we were glad to find it was not what we expected by my calculations/ I thought we must come out somewhere on the Arkansas River and though we were on the trail it could not relieve our hunger, however we marched along and felt a good deal more courage anyhow.

We kept on till about noon when suddenly a party of men hove in sight, Just as soon as I became convinced that they were white men I suddenly grew weak and had to lay down by the road side until they came up. When they came up they knew without asking what was the matter, They could see by our looks that we were almost famished. They spoke to us kindly and without asking any unnecessary questions at once commenced preparing something for us to eat. There was five in the party each one having a pack mule, but the first thing that caught my attention was two quarters of venison which hung from their saddles. Some of them lit a fire, Others sliced the venison and commenced to fry it and the rest of them got out their bag of meal and rolled out some corn dodgers, and one of them went down to the stream for some water to make coffee.

In a few minutes all was prepared and we set to but they advised us to eat sparingly at first. We did so, and in a short time set to again and made a most ferocious onslaught, This time rolls of venison corn dodger and cups of coffee disappeared with lightning rapidity the crowd all standing by and admiring the address which we disposed of their victuals.

After we had satisfied ourselves they asked us
where we had been wandering. We showed them
as near as we could the direction we had come.
They said that we had crossed the mountains where
they were never crossed before and that it was a
miracle that we had come over alive. They told us
that we were about forty miles from camp and
thirty miles from Arkansas diggings. We were then
deceived as to the distance for we were told it was
only thirty miles at most when we started. They
also gave us directions about the road/ They had
just come from the Arkansas. About twenty miles
further on they told us we could get provisions to
buy, but they said that we should be hungry again
before we got there and gave us the balance of the
leg of venison. I offered them payment for all but
they would have none of it. I thanked the generous
hearted fellows and they after wishing us better
luck on the balance of our journey left us. I never
thought I could stand such hardships/ Thirty
hours without a morsel of food and walked forty
five miles during the time and that the roughest kind
of traveling over mountains covered with timber
snow ice and dangerous rocks.

Our kind friends told us that about five miles
further on we would come to some pretty good
grass/ We got there about the middle of the afternoon and found it to be so. We camped there for
the night and the mule had a good meal as well
as ourselves. We had a comfortable time of it this

evening, We sliced some of the venison and wished for nothing else to make a good supper, The mule was also enjoying himself hugely. We felt as happy as if we had arrived in some civilized country.

We had to sleep tonight without any shelter the [spot] on which we camped being a small patch of prairie about two miles in extent with scarce any timber, The fuel was so scarce that we had to [do] without any fire, The night was pretty cold and it was not very comfortable having only the thickness of one blanket between you and the cold frosty winds. I awoke several times in the night so thoroughly chilled through that all circulation of the blood was stopped and I had to run around for some time to get up a little warmth.

Morning came at last to our great satisfaction and we had another meal off of the quarter of venison, Caught our mule, He felt very lively after his good feast. Packed up our traps and started again. About noon we came to the house that our kind friends told us we could buy provisions. It was a log hut about sixteen feet square and eight feet high. I noticed a sign nailed to the corner, "Bred for sail." Both words [were] spelled as wrong as possible, however that did not make any difference, We knew what it meant and were bound to have some. I walked into the "ranche", Every house in this place is so-called.

There was a tall rawboned Vermont woman and her daughter there. I saw three loaves of bread on a table that just came out of the oven/ The loaves were all joined together each one about as large as a pound loaf of baker's bread/ I grabbed ahold of one and asked how much for it/ The old woman quickly pulled out a scales and said that bread was worth thirty cents a pound/ It was a gross extortion but I told her to weigh it/ It was just three pounds and came to one dollar and twenty cents [*sic*]. It was nothing but wet dough half baked and left so on purpose to weigh heavy. Flour was only worth sixteen cents a pound but the old speculator knew that we were obliged to buy at any price/ I paid her for the loaf and then bought two quarts of milk from her, forty cents more making altogether one dollar and sixty cents for one meal/ It was what is called out here a piece of sharp practice.

We sat down to our meal but when I broke open the loaf my joy suddenly sank about fifty degrees/ It was as black as ink and had a rank disgusting smell made from Mexican unbolted flour without anything being put in to raise or make it light/ Hungry as we both were we could only swallow a few bites/ We drank our milk/ The water had not been spared on that either and then took our leave/ We left on the table the most part of the bread.

We continued on our way and about an hour after struck the Arkansas River/ It is here a grand looking sight/ On either side is a level prairie about a mile wide/ Rising from that is the loftiest mountain of the range/ These summits are in the blue clouds and eternally covered with snow. The one on the west side of the river is said to be the highest and it is believed by Indians and white men that it is impossible to cross it. There is a superstitious belief that it never can be crossed by mortal being. But I have no doubt that at no very distant day the enterprising spirit of the gold hunters will scorn all obstacles and explore every part of its gloomy heights once the idea gets into their heads that there is rich gold fields beyond those peaks and you could get a party of volunteers in one hour. The river here is a clear stream about fifty yards wide and running at the rate of about ten miles an hour, It is a very beautiful stream,

Our road now lay alongside the river and we soon met the wagon road and then we had plenty of company as there was a great many teams going the same way, We kept company with one team and bought some provisions of them, About sunset we turned into California Gulch the place we intended trying,[30] We were still five miles from the mining place and so had to camp for the night.

The character of the gulches are peculiar and

[30] California Gulch is a tributary of the upper reaches of the Arkansas River. The story is told that an 1860 miner gave it its name when he yelled, "Boys, I've got all California here in this pan." The principal camp in the gulch area was named Oro, some seven miles from where Leadville was later established. Muriel Sibell Wolle, *Stampede to Timberline: The Ghost Towns and Mining Camps of Colorado* (Denver, 1949), 44; Henderson, *Mining in Colorado*, 40–41.

worth describing, They generally run parallel with each other and at right angles to some river or stream, so that by going along the stream you can go to any gulch you wish without the labor of crossing the mountains, for between each gulch there is generally a high mountain.

We had a merry party this night about forty persons camped in the same place. There was nothing said till every one had his supper. Then the fun commenced, It seems they were all Pike County men. They used to say on the road that you could always tell a Pike County man from all the rest of mankind by the cut of his hat, It had a wide brim and a top about two feet high and tapering to a point. They sung [and] danced for they had two excellent fiddlers along. Drank a little "red eye," and in a couple of hours they shouted so as to raise such an echo round them old mountains as had not been heard since the flood. About midnight it all died away and we rolled up in our blankets before a good log fire and had a comfortable sleep till morning.

When I woke up all the party were in motion fires going briskly and breakfasts preparing, With all dispatch we clubbed with two more travelers and they had some ham so that putting all together we had a first rate meal,

We then started up the California Gulch a narrow valley between two very high mountains. There was a small stream of very nice clear water running in the center, The sides of the mountains were

California Gulch, date unknown

covered with a dense growth of pine. It seems very strange that timber grows so perpendicular on these steep hills, I have seen them growing some places where the hills rose as sharp as eighty or ninety degrees and the pines were perfectly straight and perpendicular. This morning we started a herd of deer and succeeded in killing three of them, They were divided amongst the whole party.

In a short time we arrived at the commencement of the diggings. Everything here looked to be substantial and permanent although it was a new place. They had good log houses to live in. Their claims were open and large parties to work on every one of them. It looked as if it was a good paying place.

In a short time I found some friends of whom I was in search, They had a claim in what was called the richest part of the gulch, They said they were making ten dollars a day. I seen their washings weighed in the evening and it amounted to what they stated. There was no such thing as getting a claim on that gulch, They valued them at from five hundred to one thousand dollars.

I was informed there was a great deal of what was called salting going on in this gulch. The operation is worth describing, A practiced miner gets a claim, He soon finds that it will yield little or nothing so he procures a little gold dust sprinkles it on a spot of the claim. In a short time some greenhorn comes along wants to buy a claim, asks for a sample. Before he purchases the miner hands him up a pan full of the stocked dirt. Greeny goes to work and washes the dirt and finds that he has found a rich claim/ There may be ten or fifteen cents in the bottom of the pan. He gets very eager to purchase/ The miner says it is better than he thought and does not care about selling/ That only makes greeny more anxious and he makes large offers two three five hundred dollars. The miner laughs at him/ Says he would not sell a cent under ten thousand and but seeing you are so eager to purchase he asks you how much money you have got. Five hundred, well then I shall let you have the claim by paying five hundred down and the balance as you take it out. Greeny thinks it a splendid chance and pays over the money at once to secure the bargain.

The sharper pockets his money with the greatest glee and immediately takes his departure for some other part of the country and you may be sure he will never come back for the balance of his pay nine thousand five hundred. The poor victim works the claim until he has eat up all his provisions and finally he has to abandon it having nothing for his money and labor but dear bought experience. I have seen many such cases as that poor silly fellow's giving up their wagon teams and almost all their provisions for a claim not worth five dollars/ You could go and take possession of as good a one at any time for nothing, but they will not believe it, They think all the good claims are found and that there is no way of getting one except by purchase.

California Gulch at the time I speak of was very scarce of water and to provide against the supply giving out they were bringing water five miles. The way it was done was to make each one of the miners work on the ditch one day in the week which made about a thousand men to work on it every day. They have now been at it twelve days. It was a tremendous undertaking over hills and valleys, The way they had to do it was to wind around over the sides of the hills having a little descent towards the place they intended bringing the water. Although it was only five miles on a straight line the surveyor said it made ten by the winding way they had to take.

On this gulch they had a regular organization judicial officers chosen and a code of laws made by themselves for their own protection, If there was any dispute about the title of a claim it was decided by miners' meeting. The way to have a meeting was to go to the president who would order the sheriff to post up the necessary notices. The meeting would assemble at the time ordered, The president would call them to order and then the trial would go on just the same as in any court of justice the witnesses being all sworn, After the testimony a vote would be taken "viva voce," and that decision would be final, If the defeated party insisted on holding your claim after that and come onto it to dispossess yours you would be justified in shooting him dead.

It was the same for any criminal offenses murder, horse stealing stealing. All were tried in the same manner and punishment inflicted in accordance with enormity of the crime. For lesser offenses the punishment was a number of lashes laid on the bare back and the prisoner tied to a tree, Generally when this punishment was inflicted the prisoner was banished and on pain of death never to show himself again in the community. Among so many turbulent spirited, all the desperadoes from the states, you may be sure that scarcely a night passed that some one or more was on trial and capital punishment was of frequent occurrence.

The bedrock in the gulch was about twelve feet deep, and it was very hard to get down as it was a solid mass of boulder stones.

That night I got lodgings with my friends,

I knew already that there was no sight for us there and I proposed after seeing all the gulch for I meant to spend all the next day on it, to go prospecting and see if we could not find something ourselves. I saw clearly that there was no use trying to get into one of the old gulches, It took too much money to buy a claim and if I had the money I should be sorry to invest it in that way.

The house that we were stopping at was a kind of store, Our friends got us up a first rate supper consisting of venison bacon, good bread, tea milk and sugar/ It looked comfortable and homelike. We got some buffalo skins to sleep on and when we wrapped our blankets around us it made a very snug bed.

The next day we spent in looking over California Gulch/ We went to the upper end about four miles/ Every claim for that distance was taken and all worked some by eight or ten men. It was estimated at that time that there was ten thousand men there.

About the center of the gulch they had built a strong fort capable of all the population. It was considered a prudent measure as there was an immense number of Indians in the neighborhood. They had also another precaution a system of telegraphing/ They would start a word at one end of the gulch and it would be passed by word of mouth from claim [to claim] until it reached the lower end the time it took to go four miles being only five minutes. It was a first rate idea/ In case the Indians made an attack in one place the rest would have warning and get into the fort.

About a mile from where we started we met about one hundred Ute Indians the first of that tribe that I had seen. They were a fine looking set of men tall straight active and intelligent looking, well armed and well clothed and in fighting apparently nothing below the white man. I have never seen any Indians on the plains that could compare with them in appearance. They are savage and vindictive never sparing an enemy taken in battle. They are brave, They are match in fighting for four times their number of any other Indians.

This body was a delegation sent up by the tribe to come to some sort of an arrangement with the whites for taking possession of their mines, They were led by the celebrated chief, "One Hand," so-called on account of having lost one of his hands in battle, "One Hand" got up on a stump and made a speech of about an hour's length. He would speak about five minutes and then the interpreter would tell us what he had said. He spoke eloquently and to the purpose, He said that their great father, meaning the President had took their fertile lands along the great river and had given them these cold barren regions in exchange that this place was now owned by them and the white man wished to drive them away still farther.

They came there without permission and took the Indians' land and gold, and not content with robbing them they killed all their game and took away their only means of livelihood. And still said he if the poor Indian the rightful owner of this soil this gold this game comes to the white man's hut cold and hungry and naked he will be scornfully turned away like a dog without any compassion or in the least relieving his wants. He asked was this justice was it humanity? He stood on his rights and demanded that the white man should pay him rent for his gold mines and that they should let his game alone, He was a friend of the white man and a friend of peace but the Indian would not bear tramping upon. He had ten thousand warriors in the mountains and if justice was not done them they were prepared to take it.

He got warmed up as he proceeded and I was so carried away by free and bold appearance, his loud manly voice and the convincing force of his arguments that I forgot entirely that it was to an untutored savage that I was listening. There was not a person who heard him but were forced to admit the justice of his remarks, Still they treated with derision the idea of paying rent to a savage. "What right had he to the mines what use could he make of them?" These are the reasonings by which they deal with the Indian. He has no rights, If it belonged to a foreign power or to white men then it would be a different thing. Their rights were respected because if not they had a chance of redressing themselves. But the poor Indian is treated with contempt, It is not worth conciliating his friendship and his enmity is despised.

It is no wonder that the poor red man so often when the opportunity offered [has] taken such fearful and bloody revenge on his oppressors. Only treat the Indians with common justice the same as you would white men, and you would never hear of those awful massacres. They are mild peaceable and unoffensive until roused by a sense of injustice and then they are perfect demons in their wrath.

Some of the officers of the gulch promised that they would try to get up some way of compensating "One Hand" the Indian, Talked to him very politely and at the same time they had not the most remote idea of paying him a single cent. Why they thought and said the idea was preposterous. There is no necessity of keeping faith with an Indian, You may make him all the promises in the world with no intention of fulfilling them, There is nothing ungentlemanly in lying to the rude un-educated savage, They do not think that although rude and uncultured the savage has a soul above their mean deceit that he is the very soul of honor and I think the most perfect gentleman of the two.

We now come to where the most extensive min-ing was done, On some claims there was twenty men to work, and it was said that they took out five hundred dollars a day. It was a busy looking scene far as the eye could reach above and below crowded of men busily to work. They were paying three dollars a day and board to laboring men that was a good evidence that the claims were paying. Game was so plenty that you could see a couple of deer hanging up on the side of every hut. It was no wonder the Indians complained about killing their game, If this would be carried on all the season the game would be exterminated. They would not be content with a moderate supply but subsisted on venison entirely, It was so plenty there that when beef was worth ten cents per pound I could buy venison for fifty cents a quarter or about five cents per pound. The whole extent of the gulch looked like a country village the houses not being more than one hundred feet from each other.

I saw the place where they were cutting the supply ditch and it was a most animated and busy looking sight. About a thousand men to work busily shoveling picking and wheeling dirt, The ditch was about four feet wide and the same in depth. There was no water in the ditch but the level being taken by competent engineers there was no danger of the ditch failing to bring the supply intended.

In the evening we entered another gulch where the claims were not all taken as yet. We spent two days prospecting but could find nothing worth staying for.

On the second night we were camping out I had been asleep probably three hours, when I was suddenly awakened by a tremendous shouting. We were alarmed and thought that the Indians had commenced an attack. We hurried quickly towards the shouting when we soon found out that the cause of the excitement was the reported discovery of new and rich diggings about five miles distant and across the snowy range. A party had just formed and were starting immediately for the gold

field. We joined them instantly, Packed our mule
and set out in company with about fifty others at
twelve at night to cross one of the highest and most
dangerous peaks of the mountains. And without
any reliable information as to the value of the
discovery.

We kept on over rocks through tangled forests
and over slippery heaps of ice and snow. The night
was intensely dark and every few moments a fearful
scream announced that some of the adventurers
had fallen over rocks or stones and were hurt. Several of them got severe bruises on that night. The
excitement grew wilder as we proceeded, A calm
looker on would have pronounced it a party of
mad men. As we neared the place their eagerness
rose to frenzy, Every man shouted and yelled at
the top of his voice. Just as the gray light of morning was coming on we reached the gulch and each
one proceeded immediately to stake off his claim
of one hundred feet.

As soon as I saw the place I knew from the looks
of the place that it was all a humbug got up to hoax
the greenys who took the bait so easily, however
I thought as I was there now I would secure a
claim and give it a trial so my companion and
myself each staked out one. It was a dreadful looking place a deep valley enclosed on all sides by
lofty snow covered mountains, the earth on which
we stood being covered by about two feet of snow,
All the party commenced building sheds for the

weather was so dreadful cold that we could not think of camping in the open air.

About noon all things being ready my partner commenced prospecting our claims. We found the bedrock only two feet deep and on washing the pay dirt could scarcely find the color. We continued prospecting the remainder of that and all the next day, with no better success. In that time we opened about twenty places and went to the bedrock in each one and I found them to be the poorest place that I had yet prospected.

The next day we recrossed the range and came into California Gulch once more. They quizzed us unmercifully about being so easily sold, and we deserved it. All but the excitement of gold discoveries will carry anyone away. Once the discovery is reported you never ask on what authority but bundle off as quick as possible to secure one of the first claims. I felt kind of flat about that and made a resolution never to go on another such expedition without having some authority for the reported discovery.

Chapter V

Failure and Retreat:
Back to Denver

WE now went out every day from five to ten miles from California Gulch prospecting but could never find anything worth trying and in a week I found out that we had made a great mistake in coming to those mountains at all in search of gold. I felt convinced that it would never be found in quantities rich enough to pay [a] working man. Undeniably there was gold in every part of the mountains but it was for the capitalist to realize. Any person who could bring money and machinery into the mountains, would have a good chance of making a rapid fortune. But I saw through the whole thing and felt satisfied that we never could make even reasonable wages in the country.

So we packed up purchased some provisions and started back towards Tarryall. We took the pack trail again but as it was broad and plain at the starting point we felt pretty certain that we would not again lose it. This morning I saw plenty of deer, One herd came close to us and I shot a fine buck, We cut him in quarters and strapped him to the mule's back. If we suffered from hunger on our journey over here we made up for it and feasted like kings on our return back. Our journey was without any incident for that day/

The next morning just as day broke we saw a great smoke ahead that greatly alarmed us for sometimes there is no escape from a fire in the mountains/ About two weeks before that there was eighteen men burned to death at Gregory diggings. We continued on our journey looking cautiously round to see if there was any danger of the fire getting behind us. We kept on for about three miles and were horrified to find that the wind had changed and that the fire and smoke was enclosing us on all sides. The densest smoke was before us but I thought our only chance of safety was to go ahead/ I thought that the fire had passed over there in the night and that its strength had died away leaving only the smoking embers. It was just as I expected/

Almost stifled by the smoke we kept on as rapidly as possible through hot ashes and in some places we had to jump over the body of a pine that had fallen and the fire slowly consuming it. In other places large trees were afire standing upright and there was great danger from their falling limbs. We were now through the worst of it and in a short time breathed the pure air and in comparative safety. Our faces were black as coal and slightly scorched and our hair singed/ Our feet were all blistered/ Although we had on good boots the boots were so burned that they fell off my feet before I got twenty miles away. The poor mule was also badly scorched and his feet were bleeding in many places. We had hard times to get him through at all. He saw that we were surrounded by fire as soon as ourselves neighed loudly and trembled in every limb several times/ He tried to get away from us I suppose to rush into the blaze. It was the narrowest escape I ever had and I sincerely hope that I may never again be placed in so perilous a position.

We made that day about twenty miles and camped at night on the snowy range. It was dreadful cold and the supply of wood very slender so we had to lay down in our blankets and shiver all night. In the morning we started down the range before daylight to get up some circulation of blood through our benumbed limbs/ At daylight we came to a small torrent where there was plenty of wood and camped there for breakfast. That day was very fine and we made twenty five miles/ We reached the park early in the afternoon.

At about dusk we were approaching the [South] Platte River and our mule which we always allowed to go before us was jogging along as usual. Before this every small stream we came to we got on his back and made him carry us across. This time as soon as he saw the river he quickened his pace and before we could catch him jumped in and went across. We were now in a pretty stew/ The evening was very cold/ We had no wood to make a fire and our provisions was all on his back. The river was rushing along fiercely and there the provoking brute stood quietly grazing on the opposite bank.

There was no alternative but to wade or swim the stream, because we must surely perish before morning without our blankets. My comrade stoutly refused to cross the stream. He said he could not swim and that it might be over his depth, or the swiftness of the current might carry him off. So I knew that I must wade across, So I got a good stout stick so as to brace myself against the current. It was a rapids the water rolling and tumbling about in great fury,

Very foolishly I took off my boots before going into the water and I did not get more than five yards from the shore and was walking very carefully for the sharp stones hurt my bare feet when my supporting stick slipped from its hold and I was thrown down instantly and went clear under water. It was terrible cold, I thought I would freeze to death. It was only about two feet deep but I had a desperate struggle and was carried two rods down the stream before I regained my feet. And when I did get standing it would be only for a few minutes when I would miss my footing and again go under, I was ducked in this way eight times before I succeeded in gaining the opposite shore. When there I caught the mule without any difficulty, got on his back recrossed the stream and brought over my brave comrade.

By this time it was quite dark and we knew the wood was two miles off so that we had to reach it anyway or I would soon freeze to death, My clothes hung around me stiff as boards, Many times before I reached that timber I imagined some part of me frozen. We got to the timber in a short time and in a few minutes had a rousing fire, I stripped off my clothes rolled a blanket round me and hung them before the fire to dry. I felt mighty comfortable as the bright cheery blaze warmth sent the blood tingling through my veins. In a short time we had some good coffee made that with some warm slap jacks made a tolerably good supper for cold and hungry men.

After supper we stretched out on our buffalo skins enjoying ourselves hugely, not dreaming of any danger when we heard the low savage whine of a pack of wolves. The Rocky Mountain wolf is somewhat larger and ten times more ferocious than the prairie wolf, but they are very cowardly and will never attack a man unless hard pressed by hunger. This time we did not feel the least alarmed, We had a good rousing fire and I always heard that wolves were afraid of fire. We prepared our rifles and revolvers to have a crack at them if they came near enough. In a few minutes they sniffled so close up to us that we could see the fire reflecting on their white teeth,

We covered two of them with our rifles fired and had the gratification of seeing them both spring high in the air and fall lifeless to the ground. At this the whole pack set up a tremendous howling and immediately commenced devouring the dead wolves/ We reloaded as quick as possible fired another volley and brought down two more of the dirty pack. As fast as they were shot the others set upon and devoured them. We now felt in a very unpleasant position/ The pack was not very large but their constant howling was attracting reinforcements every minute, and if they got very numerous they would get emboldened and probably might attack us. We kept the fire blazing brightly and fired at them as rapidly as we could load our rifles. This kept them in check and also gratified their appetite. For about an hour they swarmed around us then they began to slink away. They did not appear to be the least afraid of us and I know we should not got rid of them so easily, only for killing some and so gratifying the ravenous creatures. Their howls soon died away in the distance but we were so alarmed that they might return that we took turn about sleeping for the balance of the night. They did not come back and we had no farther disturbance till morning. At daylight we counted the skeletons of twenty wolves with every particle of flesh picked from the bones.

After breakfast we started again on our road. We knew the camp was not more than eight or ten miles distant. We had to cross the Platte once more but made sure this time of securing the mule before he got near the river.

About noon we came in sight of the camp, When we came near all the boys were standing around but they did not recognize us until we spoke to them. We made a most woeful appearance. When we started out we had a gay suit of miner's dress. Only two weeks passed and we came back our clothes hanging in shreds from our backs, our hats in ribbons and scarcely affording us any protection from the sun, Our boots were left behind more than twenty miles back and our feet entirely bare and all cut from the sharp jagged rocks. They had a thousand questions to ask us but before we would answer any of them we made them get us something to eat and a change of clothing, We did not have one for two weeks. It was almost as good as renewing life when we got new clothes and I felt as if it was worth going through all those hardships for the rare enjoyment of that hour.

We told them our story and they gave us a history of their adventures since they had been to all the diggings within fifty miles of the place and spent a great deal of time prospecting with no better result than ourselves. They had come to the same conclusion with us that the whole thing was a humbug and that we had better get out of the place as soon as possible. We had a consultation that night and agreed to make a start for Denver in the morning. But we were not to go as soon as we expected,

In the morning we were startled by a report that gold was discovered on the gulch on which we were camping. A crowd rushed down to secure claims and although we had not much faith in it we staked out several claims for our party. There was about a thousand camped there and the excitement run pretty high. The place was situated on a small stream at Tarryall that runs through the park and into the Platte River. Our claims lay on a level plain one mile away from the mountains. Although the place did not look promising the wildest excitement continued all through the day, and claims were staked off ten miles into the park.

We went to work and bought some boards at the rate of fifteen dollars per hundred feet or one hundred and fifty per thousand. The boards were sawed by hand, and that is one of the best paying businesses in this part of the country. A man that understands the work can easily make eight or ten dollars a day. Some of us went to work making sluices and the rest commenced opening the claim, We had first to make a tail ditch and turn the bed of the stream and it being a large stream it was [a] very laborious job. We got it turned in three days and then commenced digging in the center of the original bed of the stream. It was awful hard work being all composed of small boulder stone very small and closely packed together. The pick was the only means for getting them out. We worked three days before we came to the bedrock. It was just eleven feet deep/ We then commenced washing what we called the pay dirt/ We worked diligently all day/ In the evening washed our sluice tailings. Weighed it and found the whole proceeds of the day's work to be three dollars or about forty three cents each.

The prospect was rather discouraging but we should continue at it and have a fair trial. The next day we did not do as well, and we continued on for two weeks with ever varying daily proceeds, but the amount for any one day's work never exceeded seventy cents per man. We concluded that was not a paying business as our expenses was about a dollar a day at the least. So we made up our minds once more to leave the mountains and start for the States. We made all necessary arrangements to start in the morning/ I had the good fortune to find a purchaser for my claim/ I transferred it over to him for the consideration of five dollars cash.

Our horses had been kept in ranche all the time of our stay/ The "ranche", is a term used here for herding/ The herdsmen would give you a receipt for the value of your horse which could be recovered in case he was lost or stolen. On taking the animal away you had to pay him ten cents per day per head. On going down to the office at Tarryall we found that our horses were twenty miles off where they said there was good grass. They promised to send for them that night and have them for us on the following day. Col. St. Vrain[31] the ranche keeper proposed buying our mining tools and spare provisions so on the next day we brought down the remainder after leaving a sufficient supply to last us on the homeward journey. He paid us for it three hundred and fifty dollars in gold dust the only kind of money going here. We got a good price for every thing 16¢ per lb. for flour 30¢ for ham 40¢ for sugar and every thing else in proportion.

After selling our supplies four of our party changed their minds and resolved to stay another while and give the country one more trial. So our horses and mules been brought home we found a purchaser for the mule team and one single horse/ He paid us two hundred and fifty dollars in gold dust. We now divided off everything money and provisions to the satisfaction of all and about two hours before sundown we took leave of our companions on that long journey. It was a very lonesome time parting for we had good friends and true to each other in every danger and difficulty. Not an unfriendly or disagreeable word had been exchanged since we first met together/ On the day of our departure I felt the most sincere sorrow at parting from those kind friends. We might never

[31] Ceran St. Vrain was a prominent trader, pioneer merchant, and soldier in the Rocky Mountain area, especially in the Santa Fe trade and later in the Colorado country. Stella M. Drumm, biographical sketch, *Dictionary of American Biography*, XVI, (New York, 1937), 305–306.

meet again, We had perils to encounter by going home, They had greater perils to encounter by staying there. They escorted us about a quarter of a mile on the road and then left we both taking opposite directions.

We journeyed only four or five miles and then halted for the night on the banks of a clear pleasant stream. Our whole party consisted of six persons and three wagons, They were all friends and acquaintances of ours, and we had agreed to travel together. We had a very lonesome night of it could not help feeling lonesome for our friends that we had left behind.

The next day we got out of the park and I felt as though we were going to encounter hardships as soon as we lost sight of its fair level surface. Our load being light we journeyed along at a pretty fair gait, but our horses were dreadfully reduced. The mountain grass has no nourishment for our large American horses. While the Indian ponies and mules will work hard all day and thrive on it, our poor horses were nothing but skin and bones.

This night we camped with some immigrants that were going to the mountains. They gave us some news from the States and also the more fearful tidings of an Indian massacre, A large party of Cheyenne had killed a party of twenty immigrants just on the borders of the mountains. Whether true or false the information alarmed us greatly as we should have to take the same pass in getting down from the mountains, but they also told us that there was a new route found out by a place called Bradford[32] and that by taking that road we would have a better road and perhaps encounter no Indians. There was no other alternative but going ahead now so we plucked up all our courage and again started.

The teams traveled so slow now that we had a good opportunity for hunting/ I took some pretty long rambles from the road/ Sometimes I would strike into a valley walk up it three or four miles and then on returning to the road would have to cross three or four mountain peaks. The game I usually got was a large species of rabbit called the jackass rabbit/ Those who seen the hare in the old countries pronounce it to be identical with the jackass rabbit. On one occasion I got a good turkey/ He was very fat and made a capital meal.

Although we had no loads we did not seem to get over the road any faster than at our coming in. Our horses were so weak that after climbing a hill we had to let them rest for a long time/ Our average traveling was about ten miles a day. The Platte crossing was somewhat improved all the big rocks being taken out of the way so that we experienced no difficulty in crossing. I think if there was such

[32] Bradford was located some fourteen miles to the southwest of Denver at the foot of the hills behind a hogback. Ruth Beckwith, "Stage House Toward the Hills," in Ellis, *1954 Brand Book*, 67–69, and map, p. 90H.

obstacles there as when we first crossed that our teams would never have accomplished it and would have been swept away and drowned in the attempt.

Every day we met crowds of immigrants bound for the gold regions. They did not feel the least disheartened by the discouraging accounts they received from those returning. There is such a charm about the very name of digging gold. Every one thinks he will be the lucky person and where so many failed, that he may perhaps make his fortune. Fill them full of stories about wonderful discoveries and they will believe it all because it agrees with their inclinations, but tell them about the dangers and difficulties all the privations hunger, cold and fatigue they will have to undergo, of working up to their knees in cold ice water, they will only laugh at you and will not give credit to it.

After crossing the Platte the last time we struck into the new road called the Bradford Road.[33] It was an improvement on any road that I had yet traveled on in the mountains, They had a large gang of men to work grading it. They charged us two dollars toll for traveling it.

About noon on the tenth day from leaving Tarryall we came to the outside of the mountains and it was a most grand looking sight that was then

[33]The Bradford Toll Road went from Denver to Bradford via Littleton. Settle, "Robert B. Bradford," 57. Further details of the road are in Beckwith, "Stage House Toward the Hills," 65–93; advertisement, *Rocky Mountain News*, May 23, 1860.

presented to our eyes. We stood on a level plateau about a mile high. The road winding down its steep side looked from one position to be impossible for a four footed beast to descend. Far below us white clouds were sailing along and mingling with the mountains. We could see the plains stretching hundreds of miles below us. The great Platte River dotted with dark looking timber on either bank could be traced a great distance. Denver City fifteen miles distance did seem to be almost directly under us. Every building stood plain and distinct. In the neighborhood of the mountains the air is so pure that objects seemingly very close to you are four times as far off. One time I shot at a deer that I thought stood only eighty yards distance missed him and I then had the curiosity to step the distance. I found it to be one hundred and fifty yards. We all stood many minutes without speaking gazing on the scene. It was always my delight to get on high places and till this time I felt very much disappointed in never having a view from any peaks of the mountains, but this satisfied me perfectly. I grew dizzy and sick at the stomach by standing on the tremendous height.

There being pretty good grass near by in a valley we camped for dinner and to rest our horses before commencing the descent for going down such a steep hill is very distressing on horses. We chained three wheels on the wagon before starting down hill and then the wagon kept pushing hard on the horses/ The road was made on the top of a sharp hill by taking off a few shovelfuls of the top and so making it flat for about six feet. If you got over the sides you would fall down a steep precipice hundreds of feet and of course dashed to pieces/ It was a dangerous business to sit in the wagon and guide the horses/ We all tried it in turns but grew frightened and gave it up/ At last we had to take hold and lead the horses by the heads.

We could see far down below us a crowd of teams waiting to get past/ About half way down there was a place for turning out and we having the road first they had to wait till we got past. It was hard work enough to get down but I pity the poor animals that had to drag up there. The hill was about five miles long and a steady raise all the time without any breathing places. I would not take ten dollars and walk up the hill without carrying anything. We passed the teams that were waiting and before sundown arrived at the bottom and camped in a green fertile valley.

I was astonished at the change of climate/ Last night at this time it was freezing and we gathered closely around a bright blazing fire of pine. Now we enjoyed a soft mild summer night. The valley in which we were camped was covered with a luxuriant growth of grass. We camped in the shade of a mighty pair of monuments two immense columns of stone about the shape of a hen's egg and about one hundred feet high and all that tremendous weight sustained and balanced on a slender neck about six feet in diameter. It appeared as if the slightest push would send it rolling from its rocky foundation. Yet they have stood there and defied the storms for hundreds of years. The chief curiosity about them is I think in their being exactly similar, You could not find the slightest difference. They stand about one hundred yards asunder. They look like two mighty sentinels guarding the entrance to those gloomy regions. It is said that the Indians regarded them with fear and that before the coming of white men that they never entered the Rocky Mountains by this pass. Viewed at the distance of a few miles they very much resemble the forms of men, and I think it a matter of course that the poor ignorant Indian should view them with superstition and awe.

We camped in this delightful valley for the night, We were still at considerable of an elevation and the lights in the city of Denver twinkled far below us. It was a bright moonlight night, Not a cloud moved across the clear expanse of blue sky, From our camping place we could see up to the summit of those tall gigantic mountains with their snow covered peaks, At either side those giant sentinels far below us laying in the shadow could be seen the plains stretching many a long mile. We could also trace the dark course of the Platte River and the city of Denver on its banks. The murmur of falling cascades on the ear and the sight of all that was grand and terrible in nature would powerfully effect any imagination and set you to dreaming.

On the following day we arrived at Denver City, It had improved wonderfully during the two months since I had last seen it. Many buildings had been put up and others were building which would be called first class buildings in many of our eastern cities. On Larimer St. near the bridge was built a government post office and adjoining it they were constructing a U.S. mint. It had already the appearance of a substantial and permanent city.

I noticed that the streets were thronged by Sioux Indians and upon inquiry I ascertained that there was about five thousand within a half mile of the city on the river bank. It caused great uneasiness in the city the inhabitants of which felt the utmost apprehension of an attack by the savage horde. They had already organized a company of militia for its protection. On the day after our arrival they had invited the chiefs to a consultation in the town hall. Six chiefs attended and the result of the conference was that the Indians agreed to go five miles down the river and encamp. The citizens agreed that if the Sioux were attacked by the Ute "with whom they were then at war" to send a company of militia to their assistance. The chiefs left apparently well satisfied, We were also very glad to get rid of such dangerous neighbors for there was no denying the fact that they could have taken the city for there was not more than seven or eight hundred men opposed to their five hundred warriors.

Shortly after the treaty was concluded a crowd of them assembled at the post office corner and danced the celebrated war dance/ They ran round in a circle and continually kept up a loud monotonous howl for about two hours. An immense crowd of people viewed the performance.

We were encamped near the Indian town and in the evening I went down to see it. I think there was a thousand tents/ They were all planted nicely in uniform rows/ Crowds of women and papooses were gathered round every wigwam/ The place resembled a vast beehive/ They were a most dirty and repulsive looking set. Some of them were almost entirely naked and wallowing in filth and mire. We gathered from them partly by signs and an odd word that we could understand that a few days before they had a battle with the Ute that they had killed ten of the enemy and that eighteen of their own braves had fallen.

One old Indian took us round and with pride showed us the bloody trophies of the fight/ Ten gory looking scalps were stuck on long poles and each carried by a young boy. While we were looking at the horrid spectacle they gathered in a circle round the scalps and commenced a lamentation for the fallen braves. One stout Indian beat time on the tom-tom a piece of deerskin stretched on a hoop/ It sounds like a drum. The fellow beat on this as if his very life depended on his exertions, The rest went round in a circle every little while letting out a mournful howl and keeping time with the tom-tom, When the drummer got exhausted another quickly took his place and in the circle they were dropping out and getting in all the while.

I watched them for some time and then followed our old guide, He led us down to the farther end of the camp and there showed us two prisoners they had taken from the Ute in the battle, I asked the old chap by signs what they intended doing with them, He gave a most diabolical grin looked savagely at the prisoners and said "Burn, burn." I did not think he was in earnest nor that they would dare attempt so barbarous an outrage so near a civilized city. The prisoners were a fine looking young brave seemingly as bold and defiant as if he was free on his own mountainside again. The other was a young squaw about sixteen years of age, She was very interesting looking and seemed to bear her imprisonment with the indifference and calm stoicism of her race. After showing us all over the encampment we gave our friendly old guide a few pieces of money and returned to our camp.

It was now dark yet the everlasting "tom-tom," and the accompanying howling was kept up as vigorously as ever, and at short intervals we could hear a savage whoop given that would make your blood run cold. I felt the greatest sorrow for the poor young captives/ How they must tremble at heart although they shew no outward signs of fear, as they hear those demons exciting their wild and ungovernable passions until at last they get to such a pitch of fury that nothing but the blood of their captive enemy can soothe them. After getting to our tents we had some supper and then lay down to have some sleep, but we were disappointed in that the uproar made by the savages drove all thoughts of sleep out of our heads, and they kept it up without ceasing for a moment all the night.

Coming on the morning they howled yelled and shrieked like mad devils/ It was the most horrid din that I ever heard. Just at sunrise their fury reached a climax and they brought out the poor "brave" tied him to a stake made a great pile of brush round him and then setting it on fire burned the poor wretch to death. News of the barbarous affair having reached the city a great number of the citizens assembled and coming down to the Indian encampment demanded that the other prisoner should be given up to them. They gave her up immediately. The gratitude and delight of the poor creature must be imagined. Delivered so unexpectedly from most horrible tortures and death she had made up her mind that there was no escape from her unrelenting captors. That night she was secretly conveyed by a committee of three appointed by the citizens to her tribe about fifteen miles distant.

After this arrangement was made they commenced striking their tents and preparing to move down the river according to the terms of the treaty entered into on the day before. By noon not a vestige of them remained/ The place looked as silent as the grave. They were gone away without any trouble to the immense relief of the inhabitants of the city.

It was now the latter end of June and immigration was at its height/ The city was thronged with people, and the roads leading into and from the city were covered with a continuous string of teams. It looked as if all the people of the States had got demented and started off without making any preparation fearing they might be too late to lift the heaps of gold from the bowels of the earth. All were now [so] full of high hope they would not listen to a disparaging word said about the mines of the country. I can imagine how some of those same sanguine people felt about one month later/ Half starved broken down in spirit and pocket, they turn their face sorrowfully back towards "America" perhaps as I have known some of them that lost everything and undertook a weary journey of about eight hundred miles not having a morsel to eat depending on charity for their subsistence and their bare feet leaving their imprint in blood.

Seeking for gold seems to be the most exciting thing in the world. Let men only get the gold fever and no matter how well they are prospering in the world they will become unreasonable, sacrifice home means, and friends abandon all that is worth living for, for a shadow. I have seen more human misery and suffering on that road in one day than I would hear of in a year in the city of Chicago. I have seen poor fellows left a happy and comfortable home, started with some friends and a fair outfit. Now their subsistence had vanished, Sickness had laid its heavy hand upon them and the friends of their prosperous days deserted them in their misfortune. That is the place to try a true friend, He that would stick to me crossing those plains, through toil hardship and sickness, I would call a true friend and I should depend on him ever afterwards.

There was a great many objects of curiosity round the city of Denver and we spent two days looking at the sights. There was a theater in full blast with the Bateman sisters as the great attraction. The post office was opened from morning till night, You would have to get in the line behind about a hundred. There was a United States mail route now established and we got our letters for three cents. Board at the hotel was ten dollars a week and find your own bed and they were doing a brisk business, I think it was the best business going on in the city. Coming round one corner I found an auctioneer in full blast, selling as cheap and cheaper he said than the things could be bought in America. Today I saw the celebrated Kit Carson, He had come from New Mexico to pay the

Indians their annuities. He looked about five feet ten high and forty years of age a deep determined looking eye and decision in his every movement/ From his looks he was just the man that deserved all the credit of the celebrated explorations of the great pathfinder.[34]

We went into a great many stores disposing of all superfluous articles and getting our stores provided for the back journey to America as it was there called/ In our journey from the mountains all the immigrants we met hailed us in this style "Hello stranger how's the gold regions? Are you bound for America?" And indeed I think it was a very appropriate phrase/ Home or America seemed an almost infinite distance from us divided by a boundless sea. We all gave way to gloomy thoughts at the prospect of having to traverse those dreary plains again. On our coming out we had hope to cheer us on. Time passed quickly/ All obstacles were met and overcome with cheerfulness. The dreary and monotonous plains never wearied us/ Our sole trouble was to get over the miles as quickly as possible.

The method of enforcing law in Denver was of such a novel character that I think a short description of it will be interesting. There was a judge elected by the people for trying of civil cases. There

[34] Admiringly the Denver newspapers noted his presence in the city. *Rocky Mountain News*, June 13, 1860; *Rocky Mountain Herald*, June 16, 1860.

was a regular session of court held the same as in our city. One case where a friend of mine was the plaintiff will illustrate it fully. He owned a "ranche" about two miles down the Platte River and rented it to a man about a year before/ The tenant never paid any rent and laid claim to the property saying he had just as good a right to it as any body else. My friend sued him and got a judgment from the court issued in the following shape: The owner of said claim is hereby authorized to take possession of his property forthwith/ The means to be employed are that the said owner shall take as many men well armed as he shall deem necessary and take possession of his property peaceably if he may forcibly if he must/ And if there is any resistance made to this writ he shall be justified and held guiltless of killing any and all parties that shall resist this order of the court.

Another place I saw a legal notice posted on a corner/ It was to the following effect: That the undersigned had built a bridge some two months since on Larimer St. over Cherry Creek connecting the town of Auraria and Denver,[35] That certain

[35] Auraria, named after the Georgia hometown of some of its founders, was established in late 1858 at the junction of the South Platte and Cherry Creek. About the same time, Denver, named after a governor of Kansas Territory, was founded east of the mouth of Cherry Creek. After some two years of rivalry, on April 5, 1860, they were consolidated under the name of Denver. Hafen, *Pike's Peak Gold Rush Guidebooks*, 77-78.

parties having failed to make the payments on said bridge as agreed upon, That after three days they forbid any one to cross said bridge at their peril That they should have a sufficient force there and shoot down any who should attempt to disobey this order of the court. Before we left the city I heard that they raised the money and paid for the bridge.

This summary way of doing business works to a charm/ There is no resisting the court/ No such thing heard of as fining any one for contempt because no one would dare to show it/ He would be punished on the spot and in a most unpleasant manner. Since we arrived in the city there had been two executions and by making inquiries found out that there is somebody hung every week.

You must not think from this that was a hard place to live in/ I never saw a more quiet and law observing city/ I believe the severe and instantaneous punishment of crime is its surest preventive. All the murders committed here spring from the gambling table/ The termination of a dispute was always left to the pistol or bowie knife/ If one of the gamblers was killed the survivor was sure to have his neck stretched before two days and thus the community would be well rid of two ruffians. What was considered a crime deserving of death when committed by gamblers was passed off quietly as justifiable when done by other parties/ If two men got into a dispute on the street they would settle it in any manner they thought proper and if one killed the other it was all done in fair fight and there was no hint of punishment but if it was a gambler he deserved no mercy and was hung up without any mercy.

CHAPTER VI

Return to the States:
Denver to Chicago

ALL our preparations being now completed on Friday the first day of July we determined to make a start for home. About noon we went to the "ranche" to take out our animals/ Our horses were easily found/ They were very poor and there was no danger of any one stealing them.

A friend of ours who came with us did not have such good fortune/ He put a valuable team of mules into the ranche/ Now they could not be found. The poor fellow grew frantic when he discovered his loss. The ranche keeper could give no account of them but he supposed they were stolen during the night/ By the laws of the place he was responsible and could be made liable for the worth of any property left in his possession. But the owner of the mules would rather have them at that time than twice their nominal value at Denver. So he hired horses and scoured the country in all directions but it was a vain pursuit/ He never seen or heard aught of them. I am firmly convinced that the rascally "rancher" connived at stealing them/ It was said that many valuable teams were taken from his place.

Anyhow he got a judgment against the ranche keeper for two hundred and fifty dollars. The ranche was levied on and was to be sold in thirty days but the poor fellow could not remain there that long under expenses so he entrusted its collection to a lawyer of good standing in the city, and getting some friends to aid him he purchased another team and started for home. His lawyer was to send the price of his mules in a month but he never got a cent of it nor never received a bit of information from his lawyer. There is no doubt but what the latter got the money and appropriated it to his own use.

An honest man is a rare thing to be found in any place but I think it is impossible to find one at all in a gold producing country. The very fact of being where [it is] got easy brings around a lot of these sharks to prey upon the industry of the hardy miner who perils health and even life for the shining ore and no sooner does he hold the object of his desires in his hands than those blood suckers swarm around him and by one pretext or another coax his hard won earnings from him. It is a most solemn fact that in all gold producing countries the man that actually labors and plucks the gold from its hidden recesses never enjoys the fruits of his labor. Those soft silky looking fellows that never do a day's work seem to have a charm by which they attract all the spoils in their own pockets. You will see them lounging lazily around dealing in claims, taking in some poor greenhorn, and when they can make it profitable I think they have no scruple of cutting a throat.

At noon Friday we started from Denver City/ The last thing that I seen of it was a darky washing clothes/ He sung out as we passed him "Halloo boys bound for America/ Give my respects to Uncle Sam." In a few minutes we went down a bluff and lost sight of the city of Denver.

We took the old road by the Platte River. We heard of some Indian massacres on the cutoff and knew it was very dangerous to travel it. Our party consisted of three wagons and only five persons rather a small party for crossing those dreary plains. We felt dreadful lonesome/ I could not help contrasting our present position coming back disappointed from the land of gold our teams almost starved ourselves worn out by hardships and anxieties of mind. On our journey hither we were full of high hope. We considered our fortunes was ready for us as soon as we should reach the mountains/ We had plenty of merry company all as sanguine as ourselves and with high health and rugged strength/ We enjoyed ourselves hugely and had nothing to ask for.

We traveled about five miles that afternoon and camped at night with the tribe of Sioux Indians that left Denver a few days before. There was nothing to fear from them as they wished to retain the friendship of the whites as a protection from their deadly enemy the Ute. They came around our campfire in great numbers with every expression of friendship. They showed us their skill in riding and shooting with the bow.

Before it grew quite dark we saw a great cloud of dust coming from the east/ Soon we could see that it was a long string of wagons/ It was a train of about twenty wagons loaded with a crusher and machinery steam engine boiler &c. There was about twenty five men with the train and we were very glad to have company for the night/ We found among them some acquaintances from Chicago and got all the news from home in a short time. They were just as anxious to share accounts of gold mining so we told them our experiences and what we considered their prospects in the country. I think the crusher is the only way that gold can ever be got in paying quantities from the Rocky Mountains. The quartz is rich in every part and if they can only get machinery that can pulverize it there is no doubt but that they can make money in that way. We chatted with them till very late of home and friends/ They left Chicago just seven weeks before that time and considering their heavy load, they made first rate time. We all camped together that night farther than some howling and yelling/ Had no annoyance from the Indians. Just as soon as it gets dark they will not come near a white man's camp/ They know that we keep a watch and they are afraid of getting shot.

At sunrise the next morning we parted from the train each one going in opposite directions. Our road today was through the finest land I had yet seen in this country/ The grass was nice and green and about four feet high. I think it would be first rate land to cultivate. There was a good many saving hay there/ It was a very profitable business/ Last winter hay was worth two hundred dollars a ton in the Gregory diggings about sixty miles from the place.

Today we passed a beautiful island on the Platte River/ It was entirely different from any islands that I had yet seen/ The banks were bold and high and covered to the edge of the water with willow trees. There is a bridge across the river here/ Many of the immigrants cross it as it is the shortest route to Gregory/ There is a very fine house on the island but so covered in by thick foliage that you can not get a glimpse of it until you are standing beside it. It was built about fifteen years ago by a fur company for the purpose of a trading post with the Indians of the Rocky Mountains. We were now passing through a most delightful country the land rich, the grass luxurious, the blue river running clear and rippling by. It is the most charming place between the Missouri River and the Rocky Mountains.

This day we met five crusher trains and great crowds of immigrants pushing their way westward/ We would scan the faces eagerly while passing them to see if we could discover among them any one with whom we were acquainted.

The Indians were very numerous in this vicinity/ We had left the Sioux country behind and were now among the Arapaho. They are a little superior to the Sioux in habits and appearance. It seems that wherever the white and the Indian live close together that the Indian will become filthy and depraved. It is accounted for by the white man selling him whisky. The Indian is passionately fond of it and would sell himself body and soul family friends and children for to gratify his fiery appetite. The Indians used us very friendly/ Seemed to be very eager to trade with us/ They brought out heaps of buck skins moccasins and buffalo robes/ We got some of the latter from them for about one pound of sugar for each hide. Money they would not take at all but sugar coffee and meat hams or bacon they could not resist exchanging for the most valuable commodity in their possession. They annoyed us a great deal at meal times standing by and watching every morsel of food that went to our mouths/ We would generally give them some but when you gave to one others came crowding up and it was impossible to supply all their wants.

We kept ourselves pretty well supplied with fresh meat/ We had ducks and rabbits in abundance. We saw some stray droves of elk but never in shooting range. They are lordly looking animals/ I should like very much to shoot one of them. Im-

mense crowds of immigrants passed us every day.
One day I counted one hundred wagons. The average of seven persons to a wagon would make
seven hundred persons.

About sixty miles from Denver we came to St.
Vrain's Fort an abandoned trading post,[36] It was
established for the protection of the fur traders
and once had a company of United States soldiers.
Its mud walls were still standing about ten feet high
six feet thick and covering an area of about a square
acre, It stood on slightly elevated ground and a
first rate position for defense. We camped near its
walls for the night. Somehow although it was
ruined and deserted we considered it far pleasanter
to camp by its walls than to lay down on the open
prairie. It was a fine moonlight night and as I sat
there on the banks of the murmuring river listening to its monotonous rippling and seeing around
me the vast prairie its undulating surface looking
like the heaving sea, I could imagine that those
ruined walls beside me were repaired, I thought
that crowds of martial men passed to and fro, I
imagined the sentry pacing to and fro on the wall
and that I could hear his joyous ringing shout of
"All's well." All the movements passwords and
evolutions of a fort passed plainly before my eyes,
I gradually grew unconscious and awoke about

[36] Fort St. Vrain was located on the east bank of the South
Platte about one and one-half miles below the mouth of St.
Vrain Creek. *Ibid.*, 143 note; Villard, *Past and Present*, 169.

midnight chilled through, They were asleep rolled up in their blankets all around me and the camp-fire was just dying away, I replenished the fire wrapped my blanket closely around me lay as near as possible to the fire and slept comfortably till morning.

We were up before sunrise, I always liked to see the sun rising on the prairies. First comes the faintest streak of yellow light, They increase flash following flash in a quick succession, till at last the bright ball of fire itself rushes as it were from his bonds under the earth and dazzles you with the suddenness of his splendor. The appearance of the country did not change much till we got to the Beaver Creek "cutoff," the road that we took on our journey out. The grass now had a red scorched appearance and the horses did not much relish it after having such splendid grass the previous week. The road now presented an animated appearance, Crowds pushing on towards the mountains it looked like one continuous string uniting civilization with the wilderness. We were greatly annoyed by their stopping us and making inquiries, It grew to be so great a nuisance that we would not stop at all but answer all the questions we could while moving. We were compelled to do this or not make any progress on our journey. Our horses showed signs of giving out so we could not drive them more than from ten to fifteen miles a day, and Sunday if we could find a good spot of grass we gave them all day to rest.

In two weeks we came to O'Fallon's Bluffs the only spot on the whole route where the bluffs extend to the river edge. They are some two or three hundred feet high standing perpendicular from the water/ It is very laborious work for teams to get over them. The distance is ten miles/ We crossed them in one day but it was an awful hard job. We were now getting into the country where wood was scarce and got very uneasy thinking of how we could carry a supply along with us. From the weak condition of our horses we concluded it was impossible to carry any fuel and that we could trust to chance for a supply on the road.

The steady tide of immigration still continued pouring westward, and I noticed in some trains that we met whole families of women and children. The sufferings and hardships of the road was enough for a strong man to endure, but women and children were not fit for it and I think it was a most barbarous thing to bring them on the road at all.

Since we passed O'Fallon's Bluffs we have been traveling in the Cheyenne country. They are a fine warlike tribe of Indians the "Comanche" of this part of the country/ They are above begging and other low lived employments of the most part of the tribes of the West. They are said to be great fighters, have immense herds of ponies and almost live on horseback. In trading they are quick at making a bargain/ If they do not like your price they will not try to get more out of you but they will turn away instantly try a trade with someone

else and have no more to do with you. It took us
a week to get through their country and I really
thought more of them than any I had yet seen on
the plains.

One evening about an hour before sunset we
were camped only a short distance from a Cheyenne village, and a hunter drove up to our camp.
He was riding a small pony and had the carcasses
of two antelopes and a young deer also slung across
his back. After saluting us in the usual friendly
manner, "How, How," we understood from him
that he had been on the hunt all day and had nothing to eat. We gave him some tea and crackers
which he eat with a relish. He then went to his
pony and cut off the livers of the antelopes and
gave them to us/ We considered it a great compli-
ment for the Indian scarcely ever makes a present
of anything. We were out of meat and wanted to
buy some of his antelope/ We offered him tea coffee sugar but he shook his head and would not have
any of them/ We then tried money/ Offered him
fifty cents. No. At last he got his rifle made signs
of ramming down a bullet/ We then understood
that it was lead that he wanted/ We gave him a bar
of lead about half a pound for half an antelope and
he seemed highly satisfied.

After that we done a very foolish thing and it
gave us the greatest uneasiness during the whole
night/ He acted so very clever about giving us the
liver that as the liquor was passing around we

thought we ought to treat him/ We gave him a pretty good nip of whisky and I never was so astonished/ It acted upon him like poison/ In five minutes he was dreadful sick. He lay down on the ground and rolled over/ The sweat stood in big beads on his face and bare arms. He had on a white cotton shirt that some traveler had given him and he felt mighty proud of it. I got scared/ I thought the fellow might die, and if so his tribe would think we had poisoned him and have revenge out of us. I got a pail of water and poured it on his head and wrists/ That made him feel a great deal better. We done all we could for him/

While we were all busy doctering him another Indian rode over/ I suppose they had seen him coming and were uneasy at his delay/ They spoke together a few minutes/ When the newcomer turned round towards us with a smile and asked for "whisky" we shook our heads pointed to the fellow laying on the ground and told him as well as we could by signs that it would make him sick/ That had no effect on him/ He seemed quite anxious to be in the same state and said very coaxingly "Me sick too." But we would not give him any and in a short time he rode back furiously to the village. We now saw the mistake we had made/ If the Indians once gets the taste of whisky they will risk anything to get plenty of it.

Our patient was now pretty well recovered and coming to his senses/ The first thing he done was to reach for his rifle and discharge it, He had sense enough to remember that it was loaded and that it was dangerous in his hands. We lifted him up on his pony, All his regret seemed to be about having his white shirt spoiled, I could not help laughing, He looked at it with such a rueful face, It was all in white and black streaks.

We were very much afraid that the Indians would come and make an attack on us to get the whisky, We kept a strict guard all the night and I think they were hovering around us all the night but were afraid to make an attack as they knew we were prepared for them. However the night passed over without any trouble and we were mighty thankful for it. It is a very foolish thing under any circumstances to let Indians have the taste of whisky. The moment you do it they lose all confidence in you become treacherous and extremely dangerous, You cannot trade or have any communication whatever with them afterwards.

In the morning we passed through the village, The Indians eyed us savagely looking as if they would like to tear us in pieces. They did not come out as usual with their kind salute or their pile of skins and robes but kept a sullen silence while we were passing. All that enmity was caused by us having the whisky, They expected to find us unprepared and take it during the night, but being mistaken in that and finding that we were on the alert they considered that we had done them some grievous injury. I did not feel safe until I got several miles between us and the unfriendly tribe. That was the only time on our journey home that the Indians showed any hostile feelings and then it was provoked by ourselves and we were only five passing alone through this vast country of Indians.

We now suffered a great deal from heat and thirst/ The burning midsummer sun poured down on us all the long day with his fiercest beams/ Water was very scarce and although our road lay mainly along the bank of the river sometimes the road would not come near the river for eight or ten miles. Every thing was parched and withered from the fierce heat of the sun/ The grass looked as if fire passed over it/ Large fissures opened in the earth and night and day we suffered dreadfully from the intense heat.

To add to our torments just as the sun went down the mosquitoes assailed us furiously. They came around in myriads almost driving us mad by their incessant singing and their tantalizing sting. Of all the torments that ever was inflicted on poor humanity I think this is the most dreadful. There is not a moment's relief/ No matter how tired you may be it is impossible to sleep/ You may lay down cover yourself all over with your blankets but you will not be safe. Some prying adventurous fellow will find a corner unprotected and will quickly intrude his proboscis and almost before you can roll out of your blanket he will have a measure of your blood. There I used to lay for hours fighting desperately with my small enemies with blankets rolled all around me and the perspiration streaming from every pore/

At last towards morning when the air grew cool we might get some relief from our tormenters and snatch a few hours sleep. Oftentime I thought they would kill some of us/ The torture was most horrible and not to be compared to anything I ever experienced/ How I would long for some quiet cool spot where free from any annoyance I could have a few hours undisturbed slumber. The worst infested of mosquito swamps in the States is nothing in comparison to this place/ The critters are remorseless and stick to you with a perseverance and energy worthy of a better cause.

Our supply of wood was now run out and the scanty supply of buffalo chips that we picked up on the road was not sufficient to make fire enough to warm our water for tea or coffee and often times we had to eat half raw corn dodger. The least small chip or twig laying by the road was eagerly picked up and carefully hoarded until evening. We used the greatest ingenuity to husband our fuel. We would dig a little hole in the ground about four inches wide, four deep and twelve inches long, then light the fire and put on our coffee pot and frying pan/ Then we were very saving and only put two or three little twigs into the fire at a time. The instant the cooking was finished we extinguished the blaze immediately and saved the black embers for the next occasion. Journeying along slowly for we made only fifteen miles a day on an average it took us three weeks to accomplish the same distance that we had made in one week on our journey out.

We arrived at the cottonwood springs and felt as though we had escaped a death from starvation by gaining the friendly shelter of the cottonwoods. Unless you have experienced it you cannot imagine the luxurious feeling that comes over the prairie traveler on finding abundance of anything that he has suffered for and been deprived of for a long time. We rested a whole day and cooked and feasted the whole time, It made us perfectly happy to see the steam puffing out of the coffee pot and the slap jack "done brown" to a turn.

We were now about a hundred miles from Ft. Kearney, Immigration still continued to flow westward in a constant stream, Up to this time we had met forty one crushers en route for the mountains and according to the estimate we made of people it could not be much short of twenty thousand, Almost every day immense government trains passed us enroute for Camp Floyd and Carson Valley. They were mostly owned by Majors and Russell of Leavenworth City the proprietors of the Pony Express. We met the California Express messenger going each way twice a week, They always passed us at a very rapid rate.

Provisions were now getting very scarce with us,

We had made such slow progress that it upset all our calculations and now we found ourselves a hundred miles away from any trading post and had only some tea and a few pounds of meal left. Unpleasant ideas of starvation and eating skin and bone horses made us rather uneasy.

Our mode of traveling left plenty of idle time on our hands. At midday the sun poured down with intense heat so that it was impossible for animals of any description to travel beneath its sweltering rays. We rose an hour before daybreak hitched up and immediately started. We traveled about four hours until the sun grew pretty hot, when we looked for a shady place and camped. Then we had breakfast, and then for six or seven long tedious hours we had to lay still in the shade/ I had Walter Scott's works in pamphlet form and that was a first rate opportunity for reading them/ I believe I should have died of the blues but for them. About three hours before sunset we started again on the road and traveled sometimes till an hour after dark or until we found a desirable camping place. We made about fifteen miles a day just as much as our horses were able to accomplish.

One night we camped after dark. In fixing the horses I stumbled several times over a little mound of earth. In the morning I was shocked to find out that we had been sleeping on a grave/ We slept quiet and undisturbed during the night but if we knew of the lonely sleeper beneath us we would have left that place in a hurry. Thousands of little mounds like that dot the road on either side from the Missouri River to the Rocky Mountains, marking the last resting place of the adventurous gold seeker on his way to the Eldorado of the Pacific Ocean, or the weary and disappointed pilgrim coming home all his high expectations dissipated and scattered to the winds, Not regretfully he lay down to an eternal sleep in those boundless prairies of the West. As I saw those innumerable resting places of the California immigrants I shudderingly thought what if I should yet be laid down on this long dreary endless road to take my last long sleep, to make one of those lowly mounds of earth of which we passed hundreds every day. I confess the thoughts were exceedingly unpleasant and I longed more than ever for to reach the borders of civilization.

About seventy miles from Fort Kearney we came to a new established trading post and purchased there some necessaries, We paid thirty cents a pound for flour forty cents for sugar and forty cents for bacon. The house was what is called a "adobe" house being made entirely of mud the roof having a few timbers on it and then sodded, At a distance you would think it a small natural hill.

The travelers we met told us that we would find plenty of buffalo in a few days, The news raised us to the highest state of excitement, We longed to encounter the huge unwieldly native of the prairies.

The following night we were aroused by a bellowing noise/ We supposed it to be a herd of buffaloes as the noise gradually died away. In the morning we eagerly scanned the prairie in every direction but could see no signs of buffalo/

We harnessed up our horses and traveled about eight miles. We heard a low rumbling noise like distant thunder/ Then a great cloud of dust arose increasing every moment in extent and reaching up to the clouds/ We were in the highest state of excitement/ The cloud of dust suddenly cleared away and we saw an immense herd of buflseo [buffalo] only about a quarter of a mile distant. It was a most grand and imposing sight/ From the slight elevation on which we were standing this great living mass could be seen/ Stretched miles and miles away far as the eye could reach was one compact solid body moving in one direction and making the earth shake beneath them. They were traveling parallel with the road and soon we were within one hundred yards of the nearest/ We got out our rifles fired a volley and dropped two of them. One died instantly/ The other received five or six shots before he stretched himself out/ This was a glorious commencement of buffalo hunting and we felt highly elated at our success.

We then proceeded to dress our game/ One was a young bull about four years old the other an old chap about sixteen/ The young one was about the size of a large ox/ Five of us had all we could do to roll him over. We first cut off the hump considered by hunters as the choicest part. Then we skinned him. The skin is valueless in this season and we threw it away. Then we cut him up into quarters in the same way they dress beeves at home. We kept some for cooking fresh and jerked the balance, This is rather a curious process and worth describing, We tear off the meat with the grain in thin slices then throw on some salt if you wish but it is not necessary for saving it. Then hang it in the sun or suspend it before a hot fire until thoroughly dry, It is then jerked meat and perfectly cured and you may throw it in the bottom of your wagon or in any out of the way place and it will keep sweet and good for a year or more. Jerked buffalo meat salt I liked the flavor of very well but could not endure it in any other shape, I tried it boiled and fried but could not bear the taste. Even the hump what is called such a delicious morsel is as tough as sole leather and the liver as tough as ordinary beef.

The buffalo is only vulnerable in one small place under the fore shoulder, If you drive a bullet in there he will drop on the instant but if you strike him in any other place it only irritates but cannot seriously hurt him. I have known one case where a party of ten persons fired four rounds into a huge buffalo before he dropped, On examining him afterwards they found that twenty seven bullets had gone into his body.

The plain was now covered with buffalo far as the eye could reach in every direction. Hunters were reaping a harvest of game. I counted no less than sixteen buffalo slaughtered that day. The herd was journeying slowly to the westward. They travel in such a compact body that if anything suddenly forms an obstruction the foremost ones cannot avoid it, but are propelled by the irresistible force from behind into streams and sometimes over precipices. There is often great numbers of them destroyed before they stop on their headlong course.

For two days the immense herd stretched along on our right hand side and parallel with the river and extending inward far as the eye could reach. We had some glorious sport/ Killed several of them merely for the glory of the thing. Sometimes we would kill a buffalo and not take a particle of the meat. There was enough of meat wasted there that season to feed the state of Illinois for a whole year.

We now reached Kearney City two miles from the Fort/ We felt as though we were once more on the borders of civilization. I went over to a ranche to purchase some baked bread. We were almost starved living upon half cooked "slap jacks" and corn dodger. I bought a few loaves at a reasonable price. On coming out I saw a great commotion at the other end of the village/ Upon inquiry I found that a huge buffalo bull had got into a "corral" with the tame cattle. The crowd were punching him with long poles and trying to persuade him to leave. He

paid not the least attention to their hints and finally they tickled his sides with buckshot when he
left rather suddenly. They did not want to kill him
as they would have to drag his carcass away from
the village.

There was several trading posts/ We furnished
ourselves with all the necessaries for finishing
our journey/ Passed through the fort that afternoon and got down to Grand Island at sunset. We
now had our choice either to take the road through
Kansas or by continuing on down the Platte reach
the Missouri River at Platte's mouth/[37] After making
all the inquiries possible we made up our minds to
take the former route.

The buffalo were now around us in swarms/ In
every direction on both sides of the Platte far as
the eye could reach was covered black with cattle.
You could not from description form any idea [of]
this great mass of moving life. They were seemingly
entirely regardless of our presence/ All the afternoon they crossed the road going down to the
river to drink/ Sometimes they would crowd on us
so that we had to stop the horses to avoid mixing

[37] The latter was an alternate route between Chicago and
Fort Kearney to the one Young had traveled on the outward
journey. From Plattesmouth this route crossed southern
Iowa and on to Chicago, taking advantage of the daily mail
stages of the Western Stage Company, the Burlington and
Missouri River Railroad, and the Chicago, Burlington and
Quincy Railroad. Polhemus, *1859 Traveler's Guide*, 3, 12,
and map.

up with them, After we had camped about ten double teams belonging to the fort and loaded with timber passed us, They broke through the buffalo at a gallop scattering them right and left the drivers yelling at them like tame cattle.

We were afraid they might stampede over us in the night for they were unpleasantly close to us, We built a great fire trusting that that would keep them off for we were so wearied out by sufferings from mosquitoes and starvation that we were unable to keep watch. I was woke several times during the night by a loud bellowing seemingly right by the side of our camp, I always looked out to see that our horses were safe. They were in deadly fear and trembled all the night. Yet if they once got loose with the buffalo when on a stampede it would be impossible to ever get them again. The lowest spirited critter that ever crossed the plains will run off with them and it requires the greatest precaution on the part of the traveler to keep his cattle from getting away from him with the wild herd, The night passed away without any accident,

In the morning when the sun rose there was countless herds of buffalo all around us, We were hemmed in on every side. The only vacant spot of earth for miles was the small space that surrounded ourselves and horses. We got somewhat alarmed about getting ourselves and horses safely out of the besiegers lines. We hitched up drove our frightened and unwilling teams at the herd uttering the cries we heard from the soldiers the evening before, and had the satisfaction to see the huge animals give way and open a passage for us. It was like the celebrated passage through the Red Sea. For miles and miles on either side of us was a solid body of those gigantic animals roaring and bellowing the very earth shaking beneath their tread.

Sometimes a huge bull would plunge his horns into the earth and throw up a shower of earth and loose stones/ Others would lay down on their sides and spin round as if they were revolving on a pivot/ They would continue at that until they had wore a circle into the ground. Sometimes they were so unpleasantly close that we struck them with the whip/ They were awfully scared and made the most frantic exertions to get out of our way. We tickled their sides with several volleys of buckshot/ When struck they would throw their heels high in the air and strike their horns into the earth. There was plenty of calves among them but we could not get a shot at them the old ones always protecting them sheltering them from us.

We traveled all that day not camping till the middle of the afternoon/ Still that endless throng extended ahead of us far as the eye could reach. We had now traveled through them fifteen miles and still it seemed we were as far as ever away from the end. All that night they swarmed around us sometimes striking against the wagon and almost overturning it/ I awoke several times in the night and imagined the wild herd was running over us. The next morning there seemed to be a general movement of the herd towards the south. They regularly immigrate north and south twice a year, going north as far as the Canada line and south as far as Mexico.

We were now about twenty miles from the Platte River and had not seen a drop of water since leaving it/ There was a great drouth prevailing all over the country/ It was now forty days since we had left the mountains and it had not rained in all that time. The grass was burned yellow and the ground parched up. Our horses suffered terribly this day being the second day without water. We had a scanty supply for ourselves/ We drank of it sparingly as it was very warm and nauseating. That gave out before night and we were parched and choking/ An August sun poured down on us fiercely and the prairie stretched on every side of us like a boundless ocean/ No prospects of quenching our thirst or finding shelter from the fierce rays of the sun. The buffalo dotted the prairie in straggling groups, trying to follow the course of the herd, but overpowered by the heat they stopped helplessly on the prairie unable to go in quest of water.

At length as we were journeying along towards sundown almost despairing of finding relief for that night we suddenly came to a pole sticking up at the side of the road. Although we had never seen a like sign before we knew that it indicated water in the neighborhood. Quickly we unharnessed our horses and started out in all directions looking for the water, At length we found it at the bottom of a hill, but only a miserable mud hole the water green and slimy full of monstrous frogs that croaked defiance as we approached them. The side of the ditch was trampled into soft mud by the buffalo.

However bad and disgusting as it was we were glad enough to get it at that time, I took up a pint cup full and swallowed it mighty quick. We could not let our horses near it, They would kill themselves but we gave them a few pails full for the present. However we were glad to get it. We pitched our tent and camped for the night. We had a hard struggle of it that night preparing something to eat. Our supply of buffalo chips was very scarce, and we could not half boil the thick dirty water. A little tea thrown into that and some half cooked corn dodger formed our evening meal.

The next morning one of our horses showed signs of giving out. One of his legs was greatly swelled, We thought it was from the bite of a snake and that it would soon wear away. But he continued to fail rapidly and the next day he was so swelled that he could not travel any more and we had to leave him behind. I felt the greatest regret as we abandoned the poor creature on the prairie. He seemed to be conscious that we were deserting him. He made the most desperate exertions and followed us about a mile then he grew entirely exhausted and gave up the chase, but we heard him whining most piteously for a long time afterwards. It was the hardest thing that occurred to us on that long journey, abandoning that poor faithful creature, after traveling so many hundred miles and now so near our journey's end.

In about four days more we crossed the Little Blue River. There was plenty of buffalo in this locality. We stopped on this stream two days to recruit our horse for we now had only one and the poor thing was almost exhausted from pulling a two horse wagon and about six hundred pounds of equipage. We had quite a hard job to rig up fills, for a single horse an ax was our only tool. With that we chopped down ten small cottonwoods, and with ropes we soon made a temporary rigging/

Our journey now was over a splendid section of country along the valley of the Blue River. The trees were all bright and green forming a refreshing shade when the sun grew hot at midday. We traveled forty miles along this stream on a perfectly smooth road and under the shade of tall forest trees/ It made such a contrast to the broad scorching prairie on which we were scorched for six weeks that it seemed as if we had got into paradise.

After leaving that stream we had some pretty tuff [*sic*] times for the next fifty miles. Many times we almost perished from thirst/ We were sometimes a whole day exposed to the fierce rays of the sun without getting a drop of water to drink. And to add to our troubles we were afraid that our remaining horse would give out. The poor creature was almost broken down from hard work and starvation. At this time we only made ten miles a day.

Gladly we hailed our approach to Marysville/ We hope at that place to find some sort of a hack to assist our unfortunate horse. We found the town greatly enlarged since we had passed through it. It had now quite the appearance of a business town in the States. Business had been quite lively there during the summer/ The storekeepers looked stiff and important/ It looked like as if they were flush of money. We could not find any kind of critter to buy or borrow so we had to commence our weary journey again on the old style. We passed through the town on Sunday morning and made ten miles that day/

In the evening a fierce hurricane arose quite a frequent thing in the plains and leveled Marysville with the ground/ The next day we saw crowds of the sufferers on their way to St. Joe/ They had lost everything/ The only indication of a storm that we had was seeing some dark heavy clouds rising in the west about that time and a little rain but the wind was not unusually strong/

On coming to a camping ground this evening we met with a friend with whom we had traveled on the early part of our journey. One of his horses also died and he had purchased a yoke of oxen and was well pleased with the exchange/ He very generously offered us the use of his remaining horse for the balance of the journey.

We were now again on the borders of civilization/ There was a few farms on the banks of the streams. We eagerly purchased some vegetables butter eggs and bread/ We had none of these things for five months and you cannot imagine how good they tasted. We were a pretty hard looking set, sunburned as brown as Indians, our hair and beard of five months growth and our clothes all torn into rags. Our boots and shoes gave out, more than a month since. Still we lived well. We had an abundance of game, prairie chickens and quails/ They were so numerous that we could kill them with sticks. Living so well we now took things quite leisurely and was in no hurry to get to the end of our journey. Plums and grapes grew in profusion in the forests/

The weather was beautiful and only for the great drouth we might have prolonged our journey a week more. It was near seven weeks since we left Denver City and there had not been a drop of rain in that time/ Farmers were greatly alarmed for their crops/ Their stock was dying in great numbers. We suffered great inconvenience from a scarcity of water/ We always had to carry a supply in a ten gallon keg, and when that supply run out we suffered very severely. Only for that we would have probably have prolonged our journey another week.

About fifty miles from St. Joe we came into the bluffs of the Missouri River which was probably ten miles from us in a straight line/ The whole country through which we now traveled was covered with enormous large cottonwood trees/ We arrived at the Missouri River without any other accident or adventure/ Drove on board the St. Joe Bellemont ferry and soon landed on the levee of St. Joseph.

We felt very strange and odd suddenly transformed into a large city after wandering five months in the wilderness. Our return journey from the mountains took just fifty two days including all delays from fatigue or other causes.[38] Crowds of people gathered round us eagerly making inquiries about the land of gold/ We were some of the first returned pilgrims as they styled us/ We passed through the town to the lower end and then camped in the usual style/ Some of our party felt big and wanted to go to a hotel/ They could not endure camp life another hour.

There was still a few immigrants in St. Joe about setting out for the West and there was ten crushers starting in the same day/ The whole number of crushers we met on the road was fifty three/ Each one represented about ten thousand dollars.

The first thing we done after hitching up was to go down town and into a first class eating house and get a meal cooked in right style. We felt so

[38] Adding these fifty-two days and the six indicated in the final paragraph of the journal to the earlier stated departure date from Denver of July 1, the speculated chronology explained in note 1 on page 3 is upset. It is simply impossible to reconcile the few time references which Young makes.

very odd at first that we could hardly use a knife or fork, It would be more natural to go into the victuals in the old style.

We stopped in St. Joe four days and then took the cars for Chicago arriving there two days after having made the whole trip to Pike's Peak and back in five months and two days.

Index

INDEX

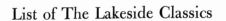

List of The Lakeside Classics

The Lakeside Classics